GOVERNANCE OF PANCHAYATI RAJ

GOVERNANCE OF PANCHAYATI RAJ

Dr. Jasprit Kaur Soni

AUTHORSPRESS

Worldwide Circulation through Authorspress Global Network
First Published 2005
by Authorspress

E-35/103, Jawahar Park
Laxmi Nagar, Delhi-110 092

e-mail: authorspress@yahoo.com

Typeset in NewCenturySchlbk by Chitra Computers

Governance of Panchayati Raj
ISBN 81-7273-284-8

Printed in India at Tarun Offset, Delhi.

Dedicated

TO THE INSPIRING & SACRED MEMORY OF MY MUMMY

Late Smt. Prakash Kaur Bagga

Preface

In every society there is disparity in power, may it be social, economic or political. But it is the duty of government to remove this. The Central Government has passed many acts to this effect of which the 73rd Amendment is one measure to bring the tribals, the most disadvantaged class, into the mainstream of this country. The Government of Rajasthan, the pioneer in bringing Panchayati Raj into effect, has given tribals their due through panchayats. It is in this context that the study has been taken up and it intend to touch upon various aspects of tribal elected members functioning in Panchayati Raj institutions.

The study covers a vast area and for collecting information or data I had to frame my own questionnaire and elicit information through these questionnaires from some villages selected on Random Sample Method. But for a major work the information has been collected through interviews and case studies under-taken by me.

My special thanks are due to Mr. Sohel Majboor, A.C.F., Dungarpur and Mr. Baldev Singh Jodha, Branch Manager, Dungarpur Banswara Kshetriya Bank, Mandav Branch for their help in conducting field survey.

I am thankful to the B.D.O. and all members of the staff, of Panchayat Samitis, particularly Girwa Panchayat Samiti for extending help in collection of data and rendering the information.

I also express my sincere gratitude to Dr. Ranjeet Singh Darda, Dean and Retired Professor of Political Science,

M.L.S. University, Udaipur, and Prof. Anju Kohli, Head (Department of Economics), M.L.S. University, Udaipur who have been very kind and helped in several ways.

I fail in my duty if I do not express my gratefulness to the library staff of M.L.Verma, Tribal Research Institute, Udaipur, library staff of Bhupal Nobles' Post-Graduate College, Udaipur, staff of Library of Social Science and Humanities, staff of Central Library, M.L.S. University, for their full cooperation in providing me books and periodicals with no feeling of any inconvenience.

I express my affectionate thanks and gratitude to my husband, Sardar Arvind Singh Soni. His suggestions and helping attitude, at all times, has been a source of inspiration to me. My daughter, Anushik Soni, a student of B.E., deserves my appreciation, thanks and affection for bearing the hardship during fieldwork and completion of this study.

My in-laws have contributed through providing me with a congenial atmosphere and taking off a number of domestic worries.

My father, Sardar Gurubachan Singh Bagga, my elder brothers, Dr. Atma Prakash Singh Bagga, S. Baljeet Singh Bagga, S. Garib Singh Bagga and my sister-in-law Dr. (Mrs.), Gajender Pal Kaur Bagga, who have always been a beacon of light for me since the dawn of my higher academic pursuits.

A number of my friends and colleagues have helped me in one way or another till the final publication of this book.

I believe that this study will prove its worth and will pave the way for further research work in this direction.

Lastly, I wish to record my thanks to AuthorsPress, New Delhi, who undertook the task of publishing this book and completed it in a very short time.

Dr. Jasprit Kaur Soni

List of Tables

List of Graphs

Contents

1

Introduction

Anthropologically a tribal is a social group whose members live in a specific territory, have a common dialect, a uniform social organisation and possess cultural homogeneity, having a common ancestor, political organisation and religious pattern. But perhaps it would be very difficult to find many tribal groups in India who possess all these characteristics.[1]

A tribe can be defined as "a social group usually with a definite area dialect, cultural homogeneity and unifying social organisation having several subgroups such as clans or sibs."[2]

According to Lucy Mair, a tribe is an independent political division with a common culture.[3]

According to the *Oxford Dictionary*, a "tribe is a group of people in primitive or barbarous stage of development acknowledging the authority of a chief and usually regarding themselves as having a common ancestor."

According to *Imperial Gazetteer of India*, a tribe is a collection of families bearing a common name, speaking a common dialect, occupying or professing to occupy a common territory and is not usually endogamous, though originally it might have been so.

According to A.B. Bardhan, the definition of tribe is a "course of socio-cultural entry at a definite historical stage of development. It is a single endogamous community, with a cultural and psychological make-up going back into a distinct historical past."[4]

According to G.W.B. Hamingford, a tribe is a group united by a common name in which the members take pride by a common language, by a common territory, and by a feeling that all who do not share this name are outsiders, 'enemies', in fact.

According to D.N.Majumdar, the definition of tribe is a collection of families or common groups bearing a common name the members of which occupy the same territory, speak the same language and observe certain taboos, regarding marriage, profession or occupation and have developed a well assured system of reciprocity and mutuality of obligations homogeneity ancestral.[5]

Thus various authors have described the tribe by different nomenclature. Dr. Ghurye named them 'Backed Hindus', Dr. Das and Das renamed them as 'Submerged Humanity', a few named them Aboriginal, Primitive tribe, Adivasi, Vanyajati, Vanabasi, Adimjati, Pahari, etc. In the ancient literature of India, namely, the *Vedas*, the *Puranas*, the *Ramayana*, the *Mahabharata*, the tribals appeared as Nishads, Saburars, Kiratas and Dasyus. They are believed to be the earliest among the present inhabitants of the country.

In anthropological literature the term 'tribe' is generally equated with the term 'primitive'. Referring to paper published by Lois Mednic in 1960 in *Current Anthropology*, Maurice Godelier mentions two sets of characteristic features, negative and positive, designated by the term 'primitive'. The negative traits include the absence of positive traits found in Western societies (non-literate, uncivilised, arrested in development, non-industrialised, non-urban, lacking economic specialisation) or the presence of those traits to a lesser degree (less civilised, low level of technical achievement, traditional simple tools, small scale). People who are categorised as 'native', 'primitive', or 'tribe' are often deprived of their rights. For instance, these people are supposed to be less civilised and not capable of knowing what is best for them. In both cases primitive societies are understood to be inferior.

Tribal habitat is a land of forest and its economy no less than its culture and tradition and its social organisation is closely linked to its forests. The tribal and their ancestors have lived in forests since times immemorial. The forests, on which they were fully dependent, were fast disappearing. Its produce that they were living on was becoming scarce. Since the forest has been a permanent abode for a tribal, he treats it as his ancestral home. There exists a sort of emotional attachment between a tribal and his forest.

They live in resource-rich region. Most forests and coal mines are in areas inhabited by them. These forests are their livelihood since much of their food and other needs come from them. They have, therefore, treated them as an environment and have traditionally reserved them for succeeding generations. But today they are being destroyed in the name of national development. They are thus dispossessed of their livelihood and are resultantly impoverished.

More and more major dams have been built in the region they live in. Many industries are established in their habitat. As a result, a large number of tribals have been impoverished. Many of tribals have been forced to migrate away from their homes and work as daily wagers and even as bonded labourers. Their culture is based on the principles of maintaining a balance between human and ecological needs and of preserving the national resources for succeeding generations. But today their impoverishment forces them to cut forests either for sale as firewood or as labourers under timber contractors and smugglers. They have thus become only suppliers of cheap raw materials and cheap labour to others. They do not get the benefits of development, while other communities far away enjoy all its fruits, but they pay the price.

This economy, social system and political structure built around these national resources have deprived them of these resources, and their impoverishment through deforestation, displacement and the attack on their livelihood have, therefore, caused a major crisis in their lives.

While studying all the above definitions and thoughts of anthropologists, it is a well-conceived fact that tribes or tribals are the aboriginal and primitive groups possessing mainly the following characteristics:

i) They are the indigenous people.

ii) They are the original inhabitants of the soil or we can say that they are the real sons of the soil.

iii) They live in the isolation of hills and forests.

iv) They are economically and socially the most backward people.

v) They are the most exploited people.

vi) They are called barbarians and uncivilised.

vii) They are the most ignored people.

Tribals of India are the indigenous people of the land in the sense that they have been long settled in different parts of the country. For indigenous people life and earth are synonymous—the earth is the rejunative power of life to indigenous people; she is their grasp of economic independence, social and cultural development, which will in turn lead to return a sense of dignity and pride which indigenous people can feel in themselves.

"The term 'tribe' has not been defined in the Constitution of India. Under its provisions, the President specifies, from time to time, various tribes in the states and the union territories as scheduled tribes."[6] The term 'scheduled tribe' first appeared in the Constitution of India. Article 366(25) defined scheduled tribes as tribes or tribal communities or parts of groups within such tribes or tribal communities as are deemed under Article 342 to be scheduled tribes for the purpose of the Constitution.

The term 'scheduled tribes' as adopted by administrators is different from that of anthropologists and sociologists. Today they recognise a tribe by the list of scheduled tribes declared by the government.

Tribals in Panchayati Raj Institutions

The tribal situation in the country presents a varied picture.

Some areas have high tribal concentration while in other areas the tribals form only a small portion of the total population. As per moderate estimate 4 per cent of the world population is divided into more than two thousand ethnic groups, which are known as tribals. The tribal population of India is highest in the world, next to Africa. As per the census of 1991, 8.08 per cent of the total population is tribal.

Table 1.1

Population and its Growth

	1981				*1991*			
	Population		*Decadel growth per cent*		*Population*		*Decadel growth in per cent*	
	Gen.	*S.T.*	*Gen.*	*S.T.*	*Gen.*	*S.T.*	*Gen.*	*S.T.*
India	361,369(lakh)	53815	–	–	770,824	67758	+22.09	+25.91
Rajasthan	343 (lakh)	41.83	–	–	440	54.74	+28.44	+27.64

Source

i) Indigenous and tribal solidarity, Indian confederation of indigenous and tribal people, 3rd General Assembly Meeting 1997, p.263.

ii) Draft ninth five-year plan for development in Rajasthan (1997-2002). Govt. of Rajasthan including Annual Plan 1997-98, volume 1, Tribal Area Development Department, Udaipur, pp.1-2.

Rajasthan is the largest state in India with an area of 3,42,239 sq. kms. constituting about 10.4 per cent of the total geographical area of the country. As per the census of 1991, the total population of Rajasthan is 440.06 lakhs of which S.T. population is 54.75 lakhs constituting 12.44 per cent of the total population.

Tribal inhabitants of Rajasthan constitute 12.44 per cent of the total state population. The percentage of female scheduled tribe's population to the total population is more than male scheduled tribe population in Rajasthan. Therefore, efforts are being made to integrate them into the mainstream society as a low caste, though traditionally they have lived in an egalitarian and casteless society in which women had a high status. Their culture is thought to be dominant culture, with its caste-based inequalities and thus women's inferiority to rank is impose on them.

It is a well known fact that Gram Panchayats had been in existence in ancient India, administering justice, looking after affairs of the villages and promoting community life. Panchayati Raj system in India is inevitable.

Under the British rule centralising the whole power destroyed this ancient culture. Mahatma Gandhi was a strong supporter of panchayat system. It was Gandhi who for the first time in the twentieth century wished to revive the Panchayati Raj institutions with democratic basis of their own and invest them with adequate powers so that the villagers could have a real sense of 'Swaraj'. Gandhi's dream of Purna Swaraj, as he thought, could be achieved only by decentralising the power to Panchayats through Panchayati Raj system. Due to deep roots of Panchayati Raj system British rulers failed in every effort to wipe out this ancient institution. With the struggle for independence rural development was given a new emphasis. In 1910, the demand for the establishment of village Panchayats was put forth in the Twenty-fifth session of All India National Congress. So in the 1920's in every province Panchayat acts were passed. But under these acts representatives were not elected but nominated by the Government. In 1932 Gandhiji started many projects for self-reliance for the villages.

According to Gandhiji, "Democracy must in essence mean the art and science of mobilising the entire physical, economic and spiritual resources of all the various sections of the people in the service of the common good of all." His concept of Panchayati Raj can be explained in the least words of Thoreau Maxim,"that government is the best which governs the least."

The Panchayat of Gandhiji's dream was supposed to attend to village sanitation, education, medical care, removal of social and economic disabilities and the likes. After the death of Gandhiji our leadership wanted his dream to be fulfilled and for this, a Community Development Programme was started in 1952. But this programme could not come up to the expectation due to non-participation and absence of active involvement of the local people because all the policies, plans, programmes and schemes for the local people came from Government officials. Social policies aimed at the rural poor were wasteful and did not deliver the desired services to most of them. It is a well-known fact that wherever there has been a community participation and involvement, programmes have been more successful.

At any time when individuals or organisations or political parties had offered any alternative to community development programme it has been democracy at the grassroots level, i.e., micro level participation, which is Panchayati Raj institution. It was Gandhiji who for the first time in the twentieth century wished to revive the Panchayati Raj institutions with democratic basis of their own and invest them with adequate powers so that the villagers could have a real sense of 'Swaraj'. The 73rd Amendment Constitutes the PRIs as self-governing institutions, and as the third tier in the federal structure of India. The Constitution 73rd Amendment essentially lays down certain ground rules with basic structural framework so that it can withstand external interference and could establish itself as an effective and strong people's institution.

In India, the roots of the Panchayati Raj are very deep. Panchayati Raj institutions in India are the prime instruments of decentralisation at the grassroots level. One of the important principles of democracy is that one should not feel powerless or feel that he cannot do much to change his situation. But he should feel that he is able to influence events and process surrounding him. We must see and analyse the Panchayati Raj system after Independence.

Poverty is the economic consequence of social backwardness and political deprivation. Participation in local administration will be helpful in enabling people below the poverty line to express and analyse the realities of their social status and economic inadequacy, evaluate by themselves their action in furtherance of their objectives.

Each person is the best judge of his circumstances, and hence, he must be given an opportunity to participate in all matters concerning alleviation and elimination of the difficulties in which he is placed, such as poverty. In the word of Dr. Mahajan, "Panchayati Raj is no doubt a bold experiment in democratic decentralisation of administration. The success of such a programme would depend upon the emergence of an appropriate leadership in the rural areas as well as the cooperation it is able to get from the people. As the experience of Indian economy shows, Panchayati Raj has yet to go a long way before it is able to find a firm root in the soil. The importance of Panchayati Raj should be obvious in a country where four out of every five citizens live in the villages and where the incidence of poverty is much higher than in towns. Thoughts on rural local Government or Panchayati Raj are thus an integral part of the concern for social and economic amelioration of the rural people.

The PRIs in India have travelled a long way to acquire constitutional recognition from a mere mentioning of it in the Constitution in the form of Directive Principles of State Policy (Article 40). It is envisaged in Article 40 that "states shall take steps to recognise Village Panchayats and endow them with such power and authority as may be necessary to enable them to function as units of self-government." This article got a mere lip service for many years before finding a place of some importance in the form of the Balwant Rai Mehta Study Team Report in 1959. In January 1957, the Balwantrai Mehta Committee was appointed to study and report the finding on community development programmes based on economy, efficiency and the extent to which the movement used local leadership.

The Government of India observed in the Third Year Plan that "The primary objective of Panchayati Raj is to enable the people of each area to achieve intensive and continuous development in the interest of the entire population. The elected representatives should be encouraged to evaluate the development of Panchayati Raj as offering new avenues of service to the people rather than the opportunities for the exercise of authority. The concept of

Panchayati Raj is not limited to the non-official and democratic organisation associated with it. Representing as it does a distinct level of responsibility of functions within the general schemes of administration, Panchayati Raj comprehends both the democratic institutions and the extension services through which development programmes are executed"(Government of India, *Third Five Year Plan,* Planning Commission, New Delhi, p. 338.)

In order to remove the shortcomings of community development programmes such as lack of involvement of local people in the project and wastage of public expenditure, the Committee recommended that the entire rural development work should be entrusted to the elected member at the village, the block and the district level. This three-tier democratic decentralisation was given the name of Panchayati Raj, which was also a tribute to Mahatma Gandhi. Thus, on the recommendation of the Balwantrai Mehta Committee on October (Gandhiji's Birthday) 1959, the Panchayati Raj movement was launched.

The introduction of Panchayati Raj system in the country is no doubt a very bold experiment. Rajasthan became the first state to pass the Panchayat Samiti and Zila Parishad Act. On 2 October 1959, Pandit Jawaharlal Nehru, the then Prime Minister, inaugurated the Panchayati Raj at Nagore and later at Shadnagar (Andhra Pradesh) in October 1959. Prime Minister Nehru praised the pioneering efforts of these two states in taking the most revolutionary and historic steps.

Research Problems

Education is considered to be an important mechanism for development in India, especially for scheduled tribes. Since these sections of our society were traditionally and historically deprived of their basic right, education was far away from their reach. For the upliftments of tribals from the Fifth Five Year Plan a new strategy was adopted and the concept of Tribal Sub Plan (T.S.P.) Area came into focus. The aim of T.S.P. is to promote the education and economic development of scheduled tribes and to protect them from social injustice and exploitation (Report :Tribal Area Development 1986-87,133). Incentives have been provided by the Constitution to these sections mainly in three sectors, i.e., education, employment and representation.

The problem of education among the tribals is related with their economic problems. As soon as the tribal children attain the age of five or six, they become economic assets to the family and help their parents in their various economic activities. Mere opening of more schools will not serve the desired purpose unless some economic incentive is provided to compensate for the loss, which these economically helpful hands render.

The rights to basic education and primary health care have been recognised as human rights in the UN Charter of Human Rights promulgated in 1948. India, being a signatory to the UN convention on Human Rights, is duty bound to provide primary health care to every citizen of the country. Problems of health and hygiene have a direct bearing on the economic and demographic aspects of the tribes. The problem of housing conditions, living space per head, drinking water and environmental cleanliness are some of the major issues which require special attention.

The focus of the present study is on political empowerment of tribals. Empowerment implies giving tribals the capacity to influence the decision-making process by integrating them into our political system. Implementation of this is the policy of reservation. Reserving seats for tribals in the political institution will provide them an opportunity to raise their grievances and other related social and economic problems in a formal manner. This is necessary in order to ensure better position for tribals in all spheres of life.

The level of the participation of tribals in political life is an issue of concern. This is because achievement of equality in all areas is seen as inseparable from active political participation. Here, political participation includes the right to vote, right to contest, right to candidacy, tribals as campaigners, tribals as members, tribals involvement in the decision-making process and appointment of tribals at all levels of government, including the participation of tribals at the grassroots through the Panchayati Raj institutions. The development programmes are channeled through the Panchayati Raj institutions. In this regard, the study seeks to answer certain questions like. Are the tribals aware of these programmes? If they are aware of these, to what extent have they been benefited, if benefited which category of tribals benefited?

Development of masses of rural areas depends upon the motivation, awareness, literacy, health and knowledge about the programmes formulated by the Government for their upliftment. Government since Independence has been working on this but the Panchayati Raj system can play a more important role in the rural development. Without effective leadership at the local level and enthusiastic participation on the part of rural population the desired results cannot be achieved.

Objectives

1. To study the knowledge of elected members about the needs of the local people and the welfare schemes.
2. To assess the work done in the field of education, health and employment by Panchayats.
3. To study the role of elected members in creating awareness among the local people about their rights and duties defined by the Constitution of India.
4. To find out their knowledge about their constitutional rights pertaining to (a) Rules and Regulations, and (b) Reservation.
5. a) To find out the constraints in implementing the programmes of development.

   b) To find out the role of Government officials in implementing the policies.

   c) To assess their technical knowledge and capabilities to implement the programming.
6. a) To assess the financial autonomy of Panchayati Raj institutions.

b) To assess the knowledge of the elected members about their financial and decision-making powers in the overall development of the area.

c) To assess whether or not the funds allocated to the Panchayats are fully utilised.

RESEARCH DESIGN AND METHODOLOGY

Research design is a blueprint of the research project in advance of data collection and analysis for the proposed research study. It is "the arrangement of conditions for collection and analysis of data in a manner that aims to combine relevance to the research purpose with economy in procedure."[7]

A research is a plan specifying the source and types of information relevant to the research problem. Any research design in research is specific to the problem and the universe to the study. In the case of Panchayati Raj leaders, it must be observed that the commitment, dedication and involvement of elected leaders can play a vital role in educating the rural masses because the majority of people are illiterate and are ignorant about their welfare.

"No socio-economic change is possible without a suitable political structure to mobilise the local people and involve them in participatory work, especially in a country of magnitude and complexities."[8]

A large number of questions arise in our mind as the role of Panchayati Raj leaders becomes all the more important in tribal-dominated areas because of the specific features of the tribal society, such as the pattern of scattered habitation, the hilly topography, the knowledge of elected members about needs of local people and the welfare schemes, the role of elected member in creating awareness among the local people, the role of government officials in implementing the policies, financial autonomy of Panchayati Raj institutions and the knowledge of the elected members about their financial and decision-making powers determine the research strategy. Keeping in view some of these specifications, the research design for the present enquiry has been prepared.

For the upliftment of tribals from the Fifth Five Year Plan a new strategy was adopted and the concept of Tribal Sub Plan (T.S.P.) area came into focus. There are 23 Panchayat Samitis of Tribal Sub Plan area. This area covers five districts of Banswara, Dungarpur, Udaipur (7 Tehsils), Chittorgarh (2 Tehsils) and Sirohi (1 Block). In these five districts of Rajasthan, we have chosen three districts, viz., Udaipur, Dungarpur and Banswara for this study.

Five Panchayat Samitis from these three districts have been selected. From Udaipur district Girwa Panchayat Samiti and Jhadol Panchayat Samiti have been selected. From Dungarpur district Sagwara Panchayat Samiti and Aspur Panchayat Samiti have been selected. From Banswara district Garhi Panchayat Samiti has been selected. These five Panchayat Samitis have been purposely chosen for the purpose of sample survey.

The Panchayat Samiti of Girwa and Jhadol have been selected from Udaipur district for studying the influence of the most urbanised and advanced district of Tribal Sub Plan Area on the political life of the tribals. Panchayat Samitis from district Banswara and Dungarpur are selected purposively because both districts are the most backward in the whole Tribal Sub Plan Area of Rajasthan.

For our enquiry on purposive sample basis, as sample refers to a small representation of a larger whole, we have chosen Sagwara Panchayat Samiti and Aspur Panchayat Samiti from Dungarpur district and Garhi Panchayat Samiti from Banswara district. The area taken as the universe of the study is thickly set with hills, plateaus and undulated land rendering the life in the area more difficult. Scattered houses along the hill ranges make communication difficult. Distance plays an important role in the socio-political development of the community in rural areas, lack of proper roads and transportation make it difficult for the people to have better opportunity to gain employment. The topographical and climatic conditions of an area are greatly instrumental in shaping the socio-economic and political activities, as the said Panchayat Samitis are not at same level of development. A Panchayat Samiti selected for the sample is shown in Table 1.2.

Table 1.2

Tribal Population and Literacy of Selected Panchayat Samitis

Panchayat Samiti Selected for the sample "Tribal Population and Literacy"

Name of the district	*Name of the panchayat samiti*	*Tribal population*				*Literacy*			
		Male	*%*	*Female*	*%*	*Male*	*%*	*Female*	
Udaipur		53981	50.78	523258	49.22	94903	17.58	11939	2.28
	1) Girwa	50972	51.28	48436	48.72	8855	17.37	711	1.47
	2) Jhadol	53167	50.76	51577	49.24	9103	17.12	937	1.89
Dungarpur		288537	50.11	287268	49.89	72529	25.14	11031	3.84
	1) Sagwara	45707	49.76	46268	50.30	12138	26.56	1777	3.84
	2) Aspur	34928	49.16	36128	50.84	6325	18.11	561	1.55
Banswara		429062	50.53	419988	49.47	82746	19.29	10572	2.52
	1) Garhi	53613	50.51	52530	49.49	12877	24.02	1822	3.47

The tribal population of these districts Udaipur, Banswara and Dungarpur is 10,63,071, 8,49,050 and 5,75,805 respectively. The male population is 5,39,813 (50.78%), 4,29,062 (50.58%) and 2,88,537 (50.11%) respectively.

Literacy is the key variable in the development of the people and their political awareness and participation. Girwa and Jhadol are parts of the most urbanised district of the T.S.P. area. As per the census we find that both Panchayats lag behind literacy as compared to the most backward districts of T.S.P. area. The male literacy of Girwa is 17.37 per cent and Jhadol 17.12 per cent, as compared to 26.56 per cent, 18.11 per cent and 24.02 per cent of Sagwara, Aspur and Garhi respectively. The picture is thus dismaying. Female literacy rate of 1.47 per cent, 1.89 per cent, 1.33 per cent of Girwa, Jhadol and Aspur Panchayat Samitis respectively give still more dismaying picture as compared to 3.84 per cent and 3.47 per cent of Sagwara and Garhi Panchayat Samitis respectively. An educated villager is more conscious of his rights and duties as a citizen of his country. Education increased the degree of participation, which is the key of development.

Rajasthan has the distinction of being the leader in atrocities and violation of human rights. As per the census of 2001 Rajasthan has also the distinction of being in the first position in achieving the highest decadel difference of literacy rate of India. Udaipur district has achieved the first position in Rajasthan urban literacy rate of 86.19 and Udaipur city has topped with literacy rate of 87.90 per cent including male literacy 94.10 per cent and female literacy rate of 81.02 per cent. Three out of five tehsils having highest urban literacy in Rajasthan are in Udaipur district. Two out of five tehsils with the lowest literacy are also from the district of Udaipur with Kotra registering 24.52 per cent literacy rate being the lowest, with 37.51 per cent male literacy and 11.14 per cent female literacy. So it can be observed from the data that Udaipur district has a varied picture in its literacy position.

Thus the Panchayat Samitis selected by us purposely represent different status of education, from gross backwardness to a progressive level. The Panchayat Samitis therefore constitute the universe of study. Three Panchayats from each Panchayat Samiti are being selected randomly for intensive study. And these 15 Panchayats selected are categorised into:

1) Progressive Panchayat and
2) Backward Panchayat

In the criteria of sample random sampling 66 elected members have been interviewed including more than 33 per cent women, for looking at women's problem for the changing needs of the time and being helpful in getting some knowledge about problems faced by them and their awareness about their rights and duties.

The researcher had used the interview schedule on the basis of which some necessary information has been collected. The interview schedule was administered to the respondents through informal interviews and discussions to elicit information relating to the socioeconomic, political, positional, reputation and decision-making profiles of the respondents.

Table 1.3
Questionnaire Administered to the Elected Members
Sample Frame and Sample Size

S. No.	*Respondents*	*Number*
1.	Zila Pramukh	1
2.	Pradhan	5
3.	Sarpanch	15
4.	Ward Panch	45
	Total	66

The Tribal Sub Plan Area covers five districts, i.e., Banswara, Dungarpur, Udaipur, Chittorgarh and Sirohi. In these five districts of Rajasthan, the researcher has chosen three districts, viz., Udaipur, Dungarpur and Banswara for the study. Five Panchayat Samitis from the said three districts have been selected, as stated before. But due to non-availability of the Pradhan of Jhadol, during her many visits, the researcher had to bring a change during the field survey. She had taken an interview of the Pradhan from Badgaon Panchayat Samiti instead of the Pradhan of Jhadol Panchayat Samiti.

The researcher had decided to select the Pradhan of Badgaon Panchayat Samiti as this Panchayat Samiti also comes in the Udaipur district of Tribal Sub Plan Area. Another reason is that the Pradhan, Bhagwan Lal Gameti of Badgaon Panchayat Samiti, is a tribal and an eminent person.

The general procedure followed for the primary data collection has been interviewing the respondents with the help of a schedule. The interview was chosen because most of the respondents are illiterate or lowly educated. This method "involves presentation of oral verbal stimuli and reply in term of oral-verbal responses."[9] Most of the interviews had to be conducted either early in the morning or late in the evening to suit the convenience of the respondents. This was coupled with our expectations of completing a certain minimum number of interviews per day.

In the light of the objectives of the study and the sample, the choice for a method of collecting data is taken to be the questionnaire. In the present study the interview schedule technique has been adopted. The first part of the schedule consists of questions pertaining to the personal information about the age, sex religion, caste, literacy, education, occupation and land ownership. The researcher herself had interviewed the respondents and noted down the verbal responses. The responses were recorded separately and separate answer sheets were prepared to record the responses of the subjects keeping in view that it would be more useful and convenient to analyse the data. A field diary had also been maintained to note down the off-coming comments for analysis. Each tool had been used with every elected member.

The questionnaires were originally developed in English and later on these were translated into Hindi. While translating, care was taken about its simplicity, intelligibility and directness. For this purpose, the Hindi and English version of the questionnaires were given to two language experts and subject experts for checking whether or not the questions in Hindi form were in conformity with the English version. The final sets of questionnaires were developed after a pilot study. In order to test the validity of the Hindi version of questionnaire, the same set of the questionnaires was given to subjects twice, first in English and then in Hindi. The forms of the questions were kept very short so that the persons of target groups would easily understand it. While framing the questionnaire care was taken to frame such questions which would elicit the information desired to be sought through these questionnaires. It was also decided to have detailed discussion with the concerned district level officials. Apart from the interview schedule technique informal interviews of post holders of the village panchayat, influentials of the village and post holders of the caste organisations, were also taken. These informal interviews provide information regarding the political activities of the village. The information which cannot otherwise be collected through the schedule technique have been collected through the informal interviews. This is because the realities are often afraid of giving information in writing to the researcher, but orally they express their views frankly. The interviews were conducted in the form of informal talks with the post holders, and influential leaders of the village. These interviews have specially been much helpful to know about the happenings of the last two village panchayat elections.

A pilot survey helped the researcher to test the validity and reliability of the questionnaire. This survey is necessary in this kind of study to establish a rapport with the people and to become aware of the area. On the basis of the survey, necessary modifications were made in the questionnaire so that the respondent could elicit the required information. Questionnaires were prepared in a simple language. Initially, there were more questions than narrated above. Some of the questions were dropped and modified after taking pilot study of the questionnaire by feeding them to a few subjects. The interview was not restricted to the questions in the schedule and many questions were on the matter to which the respondents were sensitive. The researcher had given an opportunity to the respondents to express their views on controversial subjects. A participatory observation method was also adopted for getting the additional information other than the fixed questionnaire. The additional information provided by the respondents was later on synthesised with the responses obtained through the schedule.

The first step for analysis of data was to sort out the answer sheets. The answer sheets of the first questionnaire were clubbed together and thereafter these were serially numbered. After sorting out the answer sheets, some tables were prepared on calculating the responses manually. As it was not feasible to calculate the responses manually in person, so assistance was taken from account experts to calculate the answer given in "Yes", "No" and "Undecided" on each question. As this work was time consuming, troublesome and monotonous and errors were bound to take place in calculation, it was thought appropriate to take assistance of a computer to calculate the responses of a large number of subjects.

The data and information have been collected both through primary and secondary sources. The main source of primary data was the field survey based on the interview schedule and discussion with the respondents and verification of the s[illegible] with responsible and knowledgeable person in the resp[illegible] [illegible]chayats. Secondary sources also included articles in research journals, magazines and other published documents. The secondary data for the present study were collected from the various census reports published by the Government. Data were also collected from the statistical department's report and from the report prepared by community development workers and research scholars.

The data after collection were processed and analysed. Processing implies editing, coding, classification and tabulation of collected data so that they are amenable to analyses. Editing was to assure that data gathered are accurate, consistent with facts gathered, uniformly entered and were arranged to facilitate coding and tabulation. Then after proper coding, the data were classified using descriptive statistical methods. Sellitz and other authors are of the opinion that "analysis of data in general way involves a number of closely related operations which are performed with the purpose of summarising the collected data and organising these in such a manner that they answer the research questions."[10] The data are presented in a number of tables with a brief introductory note.

The researcher had taken all the necessary precautions in the collection and analysis of data. Therefore, it is sincerely hoped that the present study shall be useful for the future researchers also.

Plan of Study

The data and information so collected have been systematically analysed and presented sequentially in chapters. The present book is a humble attempt to study the tribal life in India in all its dimensions. The book has been cuached in altogether seven chapters.

As usual, chapter one provides a brief account of the research problem in hand, the objective of the study, the conceptual framework, hypothesis, selection of the area, review of literature and methodology adopted. The first chapter gives a universal perspective about the tribals, their position in Panchayati Raj Institutions, the research problems, objectives, and the methodology adopted for the study.

The second chapter analysis the socio-economic and political background of the elected members. It also reflects on the kind of leadership that is emerging.

Chapter three deals and examines how the elected members involve themselves in the working of these institutions from participation perspective. It also deals and analyses the role of tribals in the process of decentralised planning and development, and benefits to them through development schemes and programmes.

Chapter four has been divided into three parts. In the first part of this chapter an attempt has been made to discuss the socio-political background of the elected women members as it is significant to understand their emergence, nature and social interaction process. The author proposes to examine sex, age, socio-cultural context, education, occupation, income, property, structure of the family and organisational affiliation. The second part deals with the participatory role of the elected women members in Panchayati Raj Institutions with some aspect of development and empowerment and the actual role played by them in solving the local problems and also their decision-making process in Panchayati Raj institutions. The third part depicts the Ninth Five-Year Plan commitment towards women.

The fifth chapter emphasises the importance of education in overall development. The problems range from awareness and quality issues to a missing infrastructure. There is need to create a right atmosphere at the grassroots level. The legislation could help ensure equality and justice only in a favourable atmosphere by awareness followed by education. We should try to work according to perceptions and wishes of the community, as it is they who know the best for themselves. To try and make the Panchayats the main weapon of the people is to demand their rights from the Government. The education emphasizes capacity building at the grassroots level and is expected to serve as an indicator of confidence in the strength and solidarity and bring in more development. Success breeds happiness and brings smiles.

Chapter six deals case studies of some select with elected members in detail, about their profile and of their views on day-to-day problems.

The last chapter presents the findings of the field level happenings, and on their basis recommends ways and means for effective decentralised planning. In the present study the broader problem has been examined specially in the context of democratic decentralisation and Panchayati Raj. The last chapter includes the findings of the study and a few suggestions to improve the status, position and role of the elected tribal members in the Panchayati Raj institutions. The conclusions drawn in the books are quite revealing and some of these are probably against the findings of many other studies. This chapter also sums up and concludes the study and some recommendations have been put forth.

Reference

1. Budhadeb Chaudhury, Socio Economic and Ecological Development, Tribal Studies in India series T. 148, M.C.Mital, *Tribal Transformation in India*, Volume II, Inter-India Publications, New Delhi, 1992, p.vii.
2. P.C. Mehta, *Tribal Rights*, Shiv Publications Distributors, Udaipur, 1996, p.10
3. Nadeem Husain, *Tribal India*, Palka Prakashan, New Delhi. 1999, (Definition of Lucy Mair, *Imperial Gazeteer of India*, GWB Hamingford).
4. A.B. Bardhan, *The Tribal Problem in India*, Communist Party of India Publications, New Delhi, 1973, pp. 16-17.
5. D.N. Majumdar, *Races and Culture of India*, Asia Publication House, Bombay, 1961, p.367.

6. Vimal P. Shah & Tara Patel, *Social Contexts of Tribal Education*, Concept Publishing House, New Delhi, 1985, p.2
7. Clair Selitz, et al, *Research Methods in Social Science*, Holt Rinehart and Winston Inc, New York, 1962, p. 50 as quoted by C.R. Kothari, *Research Methodology,* Wiley Eastern Ltd, New Delhi, 1986, p.44.
8. K. Shastri, *Political Linkages and Rural Development*, National Publishing House, New Delhi, 1976, p. 8.
9. C. R. Kothari, *op.cit.*, p.137.
10. Ibid., p. 171.

2

Emerging Pattern of Tribal Leadership

This chapter deals with the emerging pattern of leadership, keeping in view the socioeconomic, political background. A knowledge of the socioeconomic background of the elected members is important in shaping the nature and level of participation of members in political institutions and is an indispensable prerequisite for the understanding of the thought behaviour of its members. Emergence and development of leadership are the result of social interaction among the members of the community. Establishment of leadership pattern is fully determined by the individual's power and influence over the society.[1]

Panchayati Raj has been said to embrace a totality of ideas such as a local-self-Government organ, an agency of Government, a development mechanism and so on. Panchayati Raj leadership can play an important role in the interaction between tradition and modernity and also as an educative role in rural development. The commitment, dedication and involvement of elected leaders can play a vital role in educating the rural mass because the majority of the people are illiterate and are ignorant about their welfare.

Leadership has a pivotal role in the working of Panchayati Raj institutions. They are the 'eyes' and 'ears' of the rural people. It is the uppermost responsibility of every leader to work for the welfare of the people. Leadership should have the capacity to influence people to cooperate towards common end and also to create conditions of collective response. Thus the effective functioning of

Panchayati Raj institutions depends mainly on the equality of leadership available at the grassroots levels.

The leaders like Sarpanch, Panch and Pradhan have to play an important role of motivating rural folk to avail the facilities being extended by Government and other institutions. At the same time they also have to work as a live link between the rural people and administration. "Leadership play an important role in shaping the socio-economic and political structure of any society."[2] The role of these leaders becomes all the more important in tribal-dominated areas because of the specific features of tribal society. As the Government has acceplted the avowed objective of brining tribal people to the mainstream of society, Panchayati Raj leaders have to be extremely dedicated, committed and enlightened. "Practically, in tribal setting the leaders have a special role to play in the smooth transformation from the traditional society to the modern one. Thus, the formal leaders at the local level in the tribal region are required to be more representative, responsive and committed to programme goals."

To play a role in development of areas and its inhabitants the leaders should be vigilant and should have knowledge of Government programmes and policies. For this we have in our fieldwork worked on their personal profile. Traditional forces like caste, tribe region, etc., still continue to operate in social and political life in India. Therefore, it is undertaken that leaders might work differently according to their personal and social background.

Table 2.1

Details of the Categories of Respondents

Sl. No.	*Designation*	*Respondents*	
		Male	*Female*
1.	Zila Pramukh	1	–
2.	Pradhan	2	3
3.	Sarpanch	12	3
4.	Ward Panch	23	22

It is widely believed that the analysis of age, education, family structure, occupation, income, land holding, party affiliation, etc., are important in determining the nature of leadership. The data relating to socioeconomic background of elected representatives of Panchayati Raj institutions were collected in the present study to get an insight into the emerging pattern of rural leadership in Tribal Sub Plan Area in a changed environment. There is a significant relationship between the emergence of the respondents as leaders and the political background of their families.

In the field survey 66 elected members were interviewed including 1 Zila Pramukhs, 5 Pradhans, 15 Sarpanchs and 45 Ward Panches. Out of the 66 elected members 28 female members were interviewed in the survey to look into their problems with the changing needs of the time.

Age

Age and education are significant variables in the study of rural leadership in the Indian society. Age always has been an important factor in determining the rural leadership to take a decision. Age not only relates to the physical and mental make-up of an individual but also serves as an index of the individual's experience, awareness and wisdom in general. It is also said that the age of an individual may be responsible to some extent to make the individual take an interest in the activities. Recent trends have shown that youth have excelled and there is an urgent need to reduce the increasing gap between the youth and the old. This is needed to pursue excellence with the highest degree of efficacy.

Out of the 66 respondents 38 (57.58 per cent) males and 28 (42.42 per cent) females belong to all age group. Thus 10 males and 9 females in the age group of 18 to 30, 15 males and 10 females in the age group of 31 to 40, the age group 41 to 50 is represented by 8 males and 6 females; 4 males and 3 females are in the age group of 51 to 60 and only one male is above 61 years old. Agewise percentage is depicted in Table 2.2.

Table 2.2

Distribution of Elected Members by Age

Age Group	*Respondents*		*Percentage*	
	Male	*Female*	*Male*	*Female*
18 to 30	10	9	15.15	13.63
31 to 40	15	10	22.72	15.15
41 to 50	8	6	12.12	9.09
51 to 60	4	3	6.06	4.54
61 & above	1	–	1.51	–

Out of 66 interviewed members 44 (66.67 per cent) are youngsters in the age group of 18 to 40 years, which consists of the majority among the elected members interviewed. This is a heartening fact that tribal leadership at the Panchayat level is coming in the hands of youngsters and youngsters are taking an interest in the decision-making process.

Educational Standard

In any developing society education plays a key role in the sharing of power and the shaping of the leadership pattern. Education is an agent of change. It is an aspect of socialisation—the lifelong process of learning the attitudes, values and behaviour appropriate to the individuals as members of a particular culture. Education also promotes social change by serving as a meeting ground where each society's distinctive beliefs and traditions can be shared. Education can stimulate or bring about the desired social change. It prepares the mind to accept new roles, challenges and situations. It is necessary for the modern rural aggregate also for political and administrative reasons. Education may increase economic productivity and hence the earning power. It can improve the power of understanding, enabling a person to be better socialised, and play his role in the society in a more satisfactory way, and it may in all probability enhance the cultural level of the recipient permitting him to enjoy the fruits of various arts.

Literacy is only a crude indicator of education; it encourages entrepreneurship with little knowledge of writing and arithmetic. Literacy is the key variable in the development of the people and their political awareness and participation. An educated elected member is more conscious of his rights as well as his duties as a citizen of his country. Education increases the degree of participation, which is the key of development.

Education and high percentage of literacy will influence political participation and awareness.[3] As Sadanand A. Shetty has written in his editorial *One India One People* magazine, May 1998, "Once education becomes compulsory and universal people will be conscious of their rights and allow themselves to be exploited or treated as mere 'pawn' in the politicians game. They will then elect their leaders on the basis of character, intellect and moral excellence rather than on the basis of caste, creed, region and religion."

In the field survey the researcher could find that out of 66 interviewed respondents one female member is illiterate. An illiterate person would not be able to understand all the rules and regulations governing the institutions of Panchayati Raj. Education will help to understand the rules, regulations and fulfil the objectives of the Panchayati Raj institutions and help them in carrying out their day to day functions. Low percentage of literacy is the main hurdle in the expansion of political and ideological consideration and awareness. Illiteracy is the key problem for the development of India as a nation. Out of 66 members 28 were literate, who can only spell their names. Writing their names proves them to be literate. Literacy in the narrowness as taken in the Government policy means spelling out the names of oneself on the piece of paper but it should be defined in a broader sense as a literate person must be able to write and read with understanding and thinking and also must be able to do much more that the illiterate person can do. Fourteen members have had lower primary education and it has been observed that they could only read and write, though reading and writing are important in the context of being able to read the notice concerning the holding of meetings and able to understand the agenda to be discussed. But today there is so much of paper work in all the institutions that if one does not know to read and write, they will feel isolated. Four members have had upper primary education, 17 members have reached up to secondary and senior secondary. Only one male and one female member have secured a Bachelor's Degree in Arts. The percentage of educational standard of male and female respondents is depicted in Table 2.3.

Table 2.3

Educational Standard

	Respondents		*Percntage*	
	Male	*Female*	*Male*	*Female*
Illiterate	–	1	–	1.51
Literate	6	22	9.09	33.33
Primary (1-5)	11	3	16.16	4.54
Middle (6-8)	4	–	6.06	–
Secondary & Sr. Secondary (9-12)	16	1	24.24	1.51
Degree	1	1	1.51	1.51

OCCUPATION

India is predominately an agricultural country and its economic personality depends primarily on the developments of its agricultural sectors, but the agricultural base is very poor in the sense that it produces neither enough food for rapidly growing population nor raw materials for its industry. A majority of the population of the country live in villages, engaging themselves in agriculture; where about 70 per cent of the population is employed in allied agricultural activities, agriculturists are obviously in a majority. Agriculture has been the traditional occupation for the tribals. But as agriculture is the only major economic activity in rural areas where the rural labour force does not get work throughout the year, the true potential of Indian agriculture can be realised only when we can diversify our agricultural products, both geographically and over time.

The Tenth Plan focuses on increasing work opportunities and productivity in women farmers. Increasing women's access to productive land by regularising leasing and sharecropping of uncultivated agricultural land by women's groups, encouraging collective efforts in bringing wastelands under cultivation and providing policy incentives to women in low-input subsistence agriculture, will have immediate benefits in terms of household, food, security and women's empowerment.

Development at the village level could be seen in agriculture and the investment in inputs such as improved seeds, chemical fertilisers and high yielding varieties. In the field of agriculture, the importance of education to farmers is now recognised and functional literacy assumes greater importance. It is necessary to establish appropriate institutions, which will impart this education to adult farmers in an informal manner. It is necessary to evolve a new approach to agricultural policy based on a careful assessment of current constraints and possibilities. A sober and careful assessment of our resources indicates that both land and water will be crucial constraints in our efforts to expand production in agriculture.

Improvement in the conditions of living entails an improvement of the habitat, the surroundings in which people live. Social development of India as a whole cannot be envisaged unless we think about possible changes in their way of life. The transition in Indian economy was mainly from agricultural to service economy as in these two sectors the job elasticity is low. So industry provides more scope with technology, and especially technological competence, enhancing this trend.

"Occupation refers to not only the economic connotations but also it should be taken into consideration in other social and political perspectives. It is assessed to understand the social status and economic condition of an individual or a community."[4] Social condition of the population depends, as we have seen, on what they earn and consume, "Occupation is not only important in the distribution of status and prestige, but also a good measure of socio-economic mobility."[5]

The sample has also been divided according to the professions as shown in Table 2.4.

Table 2.4
Occupation of Elected Members

Occupation	*Respondents*		*Percentage*	
	Male	*Female*	*Male*	*Female*
Agriculture	14	15	21.21	22.72
Agriculture/ Casual labour	10	11	15.15	16.66
Agriculture/ Business	5	1	7.57	1.51
Agriculture/ Private service	4	–	6.06	–
Agriculture/ Politics	1	–	1.51	–
Agriculture/ Retired	1	–	1.51	–
Business/ Casual labour	–	1	–	1.51
Casual labour	2	–	3.03	–
Private Service	1	–	1.51	–

Table 2.4 points out that out of 66 interrogated respondents a 64 respondents are engaged with agricultural and other activities, 29 of them are engaged purely in agriculture, 21 respondents are working as casual labour with agriculture, 5 male and 1 female are engaged in agriculture with business, 4 males are doing private services with their traditionally agriculture, one is employed with political party and agriculture, 4 respondents are fully engaged in activities other than agriculture. As the villagers are mostly agricultural there is a big percentage of members having agriculture as their occupation.

INCOME

Income plays an important role in development of the life of the people. The income of a family is considered as an important criteria for determining the leadership pattern in Indian society. The researcher faced a lot of difficulties while reporting the actual income of the respondents because:

1. They are ignorant and have no knowledge about their earning during the years because they show their earning by way of yield of their agriculture produce and it is a hard task to gather correct data regarding the economic status of persons in village.
2. Agriculture is the backbone of the economy of the country and irrigation occupies an important place in the development of agriculture. Irrigation actually means utilisation of water potential and this depends on rainfall and many other factors. Income depends on the condition of land and irrigation facilities.

During field work the researcher could find that the actual land holding used for agricultural purpose is much lesser than the revenue records than the land holding reported by the respondents due to the geographical conditions and also the land holding is scattered in small pieces.

While reporting the income of the respondents the researcher has the following criteria in her mind:

i. To the source of income as the respondent is doing the job of agriculturist or casual labour or studying. If he/ she is studying then getting any benefit or not.

ii. To assess the income of all family members.

iii. To know how many members of the family are earning or contributing to their family income.

iv. To find out the standard of living and structure of the family.

It is difficult to relate education and family income. It is possible that even if there is literacy in a family, the income could be more. Income is related to a large number of factors such as land ownership, number of fruit trees and cattle, besides literacy. And it is also possible that without many of these factors, literacy could help to increase the income but higher income could be related to higher family income in a restricted way.

Graph 2.1: Income Position of the Elected Members

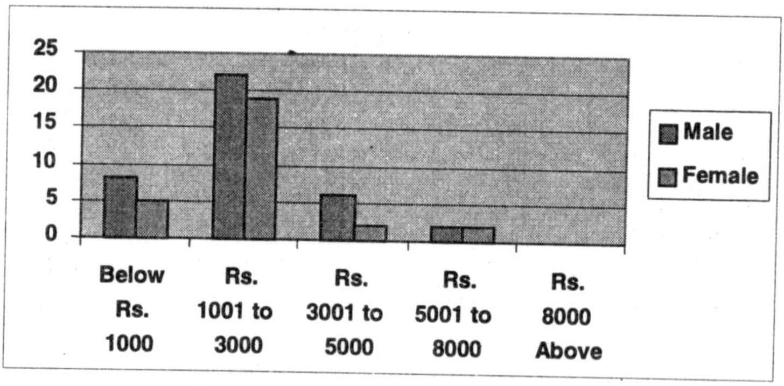

As respondents generally feel hesitant to reveal straightway their income, the figure may not be taken as their face value indicate but just as an index to the actual position. Therefore, the researcher decided not to probe for the income of the whole family, because the information about the family income is never reliable. The income of an individual is relatively associated with the income categories of the family along with the family size. If the family size is larger, the income is lesser. The researcher asked for only the monthly income of the respondents. In case of a female respondent, if she had no independent income of her own, the income of the husband or the person supporting her was taken as the income of the respondent.

Table 2.5 shows the monthly income of 66 elected members including Zila Pramukh, Pradhan, Sarpanch and Ward Panch from selected Panchayat Samiti.

In this table all the respondents are divided into three income groups as low income group which comes below Rs.3,000 per months, middle income group between Rs.3,001 and Rs.5000 and the high income group that is more than Rs.5,000.

Table 2.5

Income Scenario

Level of Income	*Respondents*		*Percentage*	
	Male	*Female*	*Male*	*Female*
Below Rs.1,000	8	5	12.12	7.57
Rs.1001 to 3,000	22	19	33.33	28.78
Rs.3001 to 5,000	6	2	9.09	3.03
Rs.5001 to 8,000	2	2	3.03	3.03
Rs.8000 to Above	–	–	–	–

In this table out of 66 respondents 54 respondents are in below Rs.3,000 group, out of which 11 respondents had monthly income below Rs.1,000 (sex-wise). The reason behind the poor monthly income is that their main occupation is agriculture and due to lack of education and their small land holding they are unable to understand and use the new technique of cultivation. For the agriculturist, education is, in addition, necessary for understanding the advantages of the use of such advanced agricultural techniques as tractors, fertilisers, harvesters and threshers. They spend their livelihood in a traditional way and not in a modern way. Of these 12.30 per cent are in the middle income group and their monthly income is between Rs. 3,001 and Rs. 5,000. This income group gives satisfaction but their percentage is less. And in the upper group, that is, the high income group which comes with an income of Rs. 5,000 and above, their percentage is only 4.61, which is unsatisfactory. This is because agriculture, the main occupation, is less, income generating.

The status of many leaders have shown that with the growth of urban life, increase in educational opportunity, progress of technology and industries, the multiplication of occupation have emerged as alternative to traditional occupation, i.e., agriculture.

LAND HOLDING

Land is the most important possession, the principle recognised wealth and it is also closely linked with power over man.[6] "Land ownership was a crucial factor in establishing dominance in the village." Tribals are dependent on the land-based economy. Land constitutes one of the most important economic assets and major means of production and income in the rural community. Even today almost every tribal household continues to depend on the land. Thus land is the only productive asset which the tribals possess. The land for the purpose of agriculture is limited. Land is the most important means of production in agriculture. The struggle between the various groups of the rural society has mainly revolved around the question of the ownership of land. The struggle over the question of land has, in fact, provided the main dynamic to the political life of the rural society in the present period. Those who fall within the higher brackets of land holding have greater participation in political mobilisation.

Land is the only tangible asset of a tribal, and occupies an important place in the tribal psyche. There are many social factors and religious rituals connected with land. So the researcher can say that tribals are socially and emotionally bound with the land. A fair idea about the economic position of the respondents may be gathered from their land-holding figure.

Table 2.6 shows the extent of land holding. Out of 66 respondents, it was found that respondents had land one to two bighas; 34 respondents had land in between 3 and 5 bighas; 11 respondents had land in 6 to 8 bighas and 8 had land above 9 bighas; but 2 respondents had no land. (Sex-wise land scenario is depicted in Table 2.6.)

People of this area own land in small pieces. These mostly lie on the slopes of the hills, unfertile with extremely low yield, the mode of agriculture being traditional.

During fieldwork it appeared that the draught, due to total failure of crops, has affected all the villages in these Panchayats. Some draught or famine relief works are in operation, but they are inadequate to meet the need of people by giving them employment. The state Government appears to have been slow in drawing viable and comprehensive plan of action for times of crisis. No permanent and long-term policies are derived to combat this calamity which is a regular feature of this area and affecting the livelihood of the people of this area. In other words, there is practically no avenue of employment available either through agriculture or through non-agriculture schemes. In this kind of situation, it is very difficult to differentiate that who is the tenure holder or the landlord and the agriculture labourers.

Table 2.6

Extent of Land Holding

No. of Bighas	*Respondents*		*Percentage*	
	Male	*Female*	*Male*	*Female*
Landless	–	2	–	3.03
1 & 2	5	5	7.57	7.57
3 to 5	23	12	34.84	18.18
6 to 8	6	5	9.09	7.57
9 & Above	4	4	6.06	6.06
Irrigated				
i. Well	13	10	20.31	15.63
ii. Nahar	10	5	15.62	7.81
iii. Both				
Well & Nahar	–	1	–	1.56
Not irrigated	7	4	10.94	6.25
Both Irrigated				
& Not irrigated	8	6	12.5	9.38

The researcher found that higher income group includes one Pradhan, one Zila Pramukh and one Ward Panch. The Pradhan's occupation is business and agriculture. Zila Pramukh's occupation is agriculture with a land holding of more than 20 bighas of agricultural land, whereas only Ward

Panch with income above 5,000 has a job with a political party and has a joint family. This also shows that agriculture with small land holding is the main factor in deciding the income.

Family Structure

A family can be defined as a set of persons related by blood, marriage or adoption who share the primary responsibility for reproduction and carrying for members of society.[7] The size of family is one of the important factors determining the leadership structure in Indian villages. Several studies have indicated the relationship between rural leadership and the size of the family. Family structure is a well discussed subject and generally the difference is nuclear family and joint family is made by industrial and agricultural society. Many political scientists say that joint family prevails and dominates agricultural society and adjustment, and understanding is the key in joint family, whereas nuclear family is the fruit of industrialisation where movement, mobility, self-expression among its members are frequent and have better opportunities and more freedom of work. In recent times the importance of the joint family has gradually declined, "the joint family is said to be weakening."[8] The term nuclear family is well chosen, since this type of family serves as the nucleus, upon which larger family groups are built. A nuclear family is a universal social phenomenon. The universality of the nuclear family does not mean that family structure is everywhere the same. May it be nuclear or joint, family planning has a big role to play in the overall development of the family.

Although the family planning programmes are in operation yet it is observed that no remarkable change in social and economic development, no serious governmental intervention and no significant social and political actions by the political parties would have influenced the people about the family planning. There should be more thrust on decentralised administration of education, health and family welfare services under the Panchayati Raj. It can be instrumental in overall improvement.

Graph 2.2

Type of Family

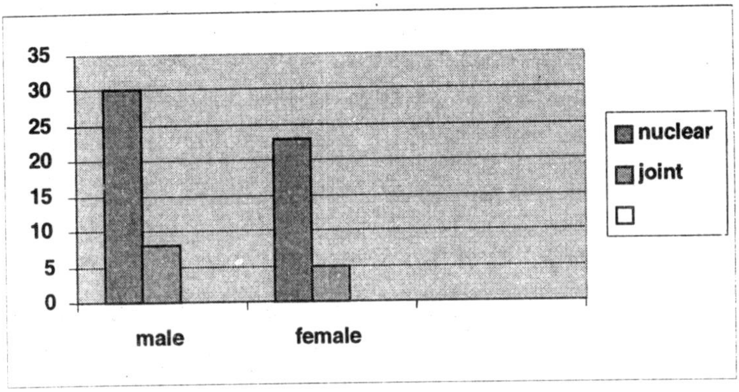

In the field survey the researcher found that out of 66 interrogated respondents 53 respondents were from nuclear family and 13 were from joint family.

Tribal society is traditionally a nuclear family society, which can be observed in the Table 2.7. It is due to that in every family when a boy is married he is given a house built for him and is separated from the day he is married. This plays a great role in economic condition and development because land and other belongings are also divided among the family members.

Table 2.7

Size of Family

Type	*Respondents*		*Percentage*	
	Male	*Female*	*Male*	*Female*
Small family	7	8	10.60	12.12
Medium family	23	14	34.84	21.21
Large family	8	6	12.12	9.09

Marital Status

When we look in the past we see that child marriage and marriage at an early age prevailed in rural society and as well as in the civilised urban society. This can be implied that the takeover of family responsibility was the main factor behind this thinking, and education was not considered to be important. But today people in rural areas have changed in their thinking and child marriage is a distinct thing to be found. When asked about child marriage and widow marriage, respondents said that there is no child marriage nowadays. Regarding widow marriage they responded that widow marriage was not a taboo in tribals and a widow can marry under 'Natra System'. It was observed during the field survey that in every village only old-age women were widows (but a rare young widow was seen). They were given full economic security which was a deciding factor in participational attitudes.

It is believed that a married person is mature, responsible and dutiful in his role performance in the society. Therefore, the marital status is considered as a determining factor for performing the assigned role effectively in the public affairs and it affects the rural leadership pattern. Out of 66 respondents 63 respondents were married, 2 were widows, one was widower and no one was unmarried. Out of 38 male respondents, 37 were married, one was a widower. Out of 28 female respondents 26 were married and 2 were widows. (Percentage-wise marital status of male and female is depicted in Table 2.8.)

Table 2.8

Marital Status of the Elected Members

Particulars	*Respondents*		*Percentage*	
	Male	*Female*	*Male*	*Female*
Married	37	26	56.06	39.39
Widow	–	2	–	3.03
Widower (unmarried)	1	–	1.51	–

In the field survey the researcher found that there were widows only in higher age group. During the field survey, one of the reasons for this was asked—Why there are no widows in younger age group? The answer was that widows were remarried under Natra System. Some of the respondents said that this Natra System was a social evil, sometime back when the married women used to change their husbands very freely. But nowadays this system is restricted to only widow remarriage.

Party Affiliation

The political party affiliation may have an influence on the participation of an individual in political activities. Panchayati Raj institutions are responsible for managing the local public affairs, but the involvement of political parties at the grassroots level would divert their attention from local problems to the national problems. The party's composition, organisation and ideology influence political affiliation of a person, and its identification refers to a person's psychological attachment to it.

By asking the question about party affiliation it was found that 4 male and 11 female respondents were not affiliated to any party, but 34 male, 17 female respondents were affiliated with different parties as 27 male and 13 female respondents were affiliated to Congress and 7 males and 15 females are affiliated to BJP (percentage-wise the actual scenario is depicted in Table 2.9).

Table 2.9
Party Affiliation

Particulars	*Respondents*		*Percentage*	
	Male	*Female*	*Male*	*Female*
Not affiliated	4	11	6.15	16.92
Congress I	27	13	41.54	18.46
Bhartiya Janata Party	7	4	10.77	6.15
Total	38	28	58.46	41.53

Party affiliation can be seen as one of the variables of participatory attitude. The political party affiliation may have an influence on the participation of an individual in political activities.'[9] Women in Indian polity show less interest in affiliating themselves to any political party because of their preoccupation with domestic functions.

Graph 2. 3:
Party Affiliation

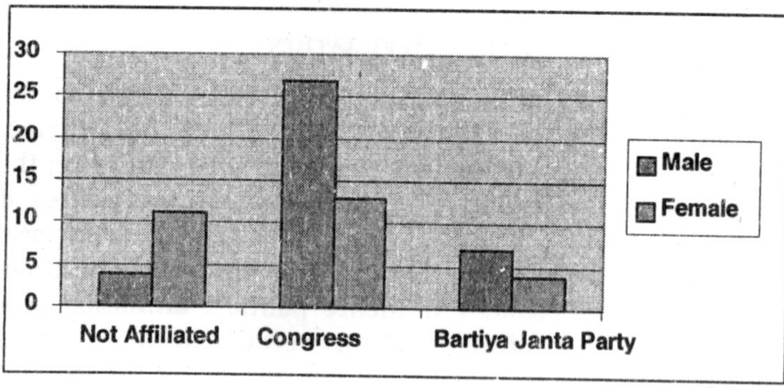

During the field survey the respondents were asked: Why are they not affiliated to any party? Most of them answered that political parties approach them only at the time of election. The indistinctness of party membership is a good indicator of the ambiguous nature of our parties. So they are only interested in their vote bank and are ignorant about the difficulties, which the local people face.

Concluding Observations

Panchayati Raj is the new vehicle of local self-government and of development in the district. Membership of PRI's serve a dual purpose in developing the personality of an individual. On the one hand, through these institutions, he is able to relate himself to the political system and at the same time develop a participant citizenship syndrome. On becoming a member of an institution, the citizen feels protected and close to the institutions of politics and Government. He develops self-confidence that is a prerequisite of a modern citizen. PRI's teach individuals the basics of a democratic system and how to perform a mediating role between the individual and the government.

References

1. Charles P. Loomis, *Social Systems: Essay on the Persistence and Change,* Princeton, New Jersey, 1963.
2. Udai Pareek and S.K. Reddy, *Studies in Indian Rural Leadership—A Review, Studies on Rural Leadership,* Udai Pareek Delhi, Behavioural Science Centre, 1966, pp.101-112.
3. Anil Kumar Singh, *Approach to Tribal Development,* Sarup and Sons, New Delhi, 1994, p.123.
4. Shamser Singh Malik, *The New Panchayati Raj,* Aalekh Publishers, Jaipur, 2002.
5. S.K. Goyal, the study of scheduled caste students of College Eastern UP, Research Project sponsored by Indian Council of Social Science Research, New Delhi, 1973
6. Louis Dumont, *Homo Hierarchicus,* Vikas Publication, Bangalore, 1966, p.126.
7. Richard T. Schaefer, *Sociology International Edition,* McGraw-Hill, Inc., New York, 1989, p.321.
8. M. N. Srinivas, *Religion and Society among Coorgs of South Indian,* Ch. 5, The cult of the okka.
9. Jasprit Kaur Soni, *Introspection of Tribal Development,* Sonali Publications, New Delhi, 2004.

3

Dimensions of Participation

Honesty, hard work and integrity along with consistent efforts are the essential requirements to achieve success. The fundamental principle of democracy is political equality, the idea that each person carries the same weight in political decision making. We would react in this way because equality of citizenship has always been central to the democratic ideal. Democracy is a way of making decision in which each person has one and only one voice. It means people deliberate about their common problems and concerns as equal. Any other arrangement would violate our belief in the intrinsic worth of the individual and would fail to ensure that the Government would pay equal attention to the values and interests of all citizens.[1]

Power is a wider term, which includes political, economic and other variations. It is simply the probability that man will act as another man wishes. While defining power, Max Weber observes, "Power is the probability that one actor within a social relationship will be in a position to carryout his own will despite resistence."[2] With the establishment of PRIs, the people at the village level are entrusted with the power to participate freely in the process of their growth and development. According to Indira Gandhi, Panchayats are formed by the people of the villages, so the control should be in their hands. We should understand that Panchayats are a combination of all kind of powers of the village people.[3]

Political participation is the backbone of a democratic system. Participation can only exist where people have common interest. According to Riggs, "Increasing participation or involvement of the citizens in state activities, in power calculations and consequences is the process of politicisation of any state or country."[4]

According to many thinkers participation is essential for mass-mobilisation in theory of political development. Huntington said, "Modernisation means mass-mobilisation, mass-mobilisation means increased political participation; and increased political participation is the key element of political development."[5]

Political participation's characteristic are further explained in definitions given by some thinkers, "Participation includes people's involvement in decision making process, in implementing programmes, sharing in the benefits of development programmes, and thus involvement in efforts to evaluate such programmes."[6]

Panchayats are meant to secure the participation of the rural people in the various activities of the rural sector. The involvement of the people in planning at the village level is bound to arouse consciousness in them. The aim of PRIs is granting the people a significant role and to work for possible political responsibility. Such participation in planning will raise the level of people's consciousness of their rights and responsibilities and will be helpful in social change. People's involvement through Panchayats in planning would result in better and more efficient planning, because they have a better perception of their needs, which would be useful in the identification, formulation and selection of schemes and programmes of local importance. They are better acquainted with local resources, and this knowledge would be helpful in collection of reliable data, evaluation and monitoring of project for their betterment. People's involvement in planning will enhance their awareness and would be helpful in making them more active and assertive about problems coming in their way.

Tribal societies in our country have a very ancient history and heritage of their own. Tribals of India have their own cultural, religious, social, economic and political structure since centuries. Nature, environment and ecology affect their lives very much. Their religious beliefs and practices are all influenced and developed around the environment and ecology which are their life-giving forces. The general people due to their beliefs and rituals call these tribals as junglee, barbarious and to some they are animals.

During field survey questions regarding behaviour of the general people towards them were asked; most of them answered that they are getting equal treatment but some high caste treat them as untouchable nowadays.

It is a fact that tribals have been able to find a new identity as representatives with equal status; they are able to participate in the work of Panchayats which affect the whole rural communities. This is certainly a step forward.

To evaluate participation of elected members some variables are to be taken into account: party membership, holding office in a party, members as electorates, members contesting elections, canvassing, members attendance in meetings, participation in committees, moving resolutions, taking part in discussions, their relations with the electorates of the constituency, participation in decision making, implementation of the decisions taken. It is an established fact that no developmental scheme can be effectively implemented if Panchayats do not have administrative control over the agencies. The nation's development is dependent on its leadership.

Leaders are the communication central system of the community or the group. The leaders are catalysts of democratic process and their attitudes reflect and define their role in national and regional economies. Actions of the political leaders reflect the common people in many ways, and their actions are changed according to needs at every step of political process by the energy, reaction and demand of active and less privileged people. The primary work of leadership is to release body, mind, heart and spirit towards great purposes. Good governance, development and leadership could also be helpful in the mission. Elected members stimulate an interest in politics and public affairs and increase participation. They communicate to people their worth and potential so clearly that they are inspired to see it in themselves. They facilitate the way for helping people to optimise their capacities and potential. They allow others to fulfil their purpose and contribution for the benefit of both individual and organisation. These principles are the foundation for creating lives.

Economic and social interests and conditions influence the voting behaviour of majority of the people, so we can say that support and respect cannot be assumed, they need to be earned. We cannot say that most people are obviously influenced by their own immediate interests, while casting their vote, but there is relationship between people's voting behaviour and their economic and social levels. Many people vote as they think will benefit most immediately their pocket, their caste or community and furthermore the needs of the area they belong to. People who are active in politics and seek their individual and collective (community and area) interests through the political party can play a leader's role because one lone individual's character can make a difference in his or her circle of influence. Few people pay attention to the working of Government, and one who can analyse the working of Government for some time can become a leader and can render voice to the needs of the locality and community because it is said that "The wheel that squeaks, gets the grease." So we can say that collective voice can pave the way for development. The mandate to any party for rule and governance is entirely for the welfare of the people and is not for pleasing people. The important need is to generate in the local community the feeling that a Panchayat can shape development activity.

We can all see ourselves as catalysts both at home and at work. For leaders who optimise their work, this is the key to sustained success. There is a serious move towards exploring as to what will be the best possible way of doing it.

Programmes and Schemes

The people of India cannot be benefited without substantial improvement in enforcement of law, infrastructure, education, health care and new opportunities for employment. The role of Government should be to enforce and implement the law to maximise economic opportunities to the citizens of India and equip them through education to take advantage of all the opportunities coming in the way. A level of development for the sake of greater equality of distribution should be accepted by the Government.

It is a universally accepted fact that economic upliftment will bring improvement in the life of scheduled caste and tribes. As also it is mentioned in the Indian Constitution under Article 46, "the state shall promote with special care, the educational and economic interests of the weaker sections of the people and in particular of the scheduled caste and the scheduled tribes and shall protect them from injustice and all form of exploitation." The Government of India gave them some relief in the form of reservation and Integrated Tribal Development Programmes. India's policy is governed by national interest only. If meaningful steps to establish coordination between procedures and time-frame implementation of measures are taken, they would take care of all the woes.

The basic objectives of Five Year Plans have been the attainment of economic self-reliance through a significant set-up in the rate of growth of the economy, raising the living standards of the people, provision of employment opportunities and basic social service. In the Fifth Plan for the first time a strategy of earmarking funds for the development of scheduled tribes was evolved. For the scheduled tribes, because of their population concentration in specific areas, the instrument of Tribal Sub Plan was developed to ensure flow of benefits from sectoral programmes and to provide an integrated delivery of service in the tribal areas. In the guideline to the state Government the modalities of quantifying funds from identifiable programmes and where necessary tailoring them to the needs of the tribal people and areas, were issued. Accordingly separate sub-plans were formulated covering 63 per cent of the tribal population in the country in 16 states and 2 union territories.[7] During the Fifth Plan with the objective of an integrated development of the entire tribal area in the country with two long-term objectives, viz., (a) to narrow the gap between the levels of development in the tribal and other areas; and (b) to improve the quality of life of the tribal communities. This new strategy was adopted in 1974-75 and a new 'Tribal Area Development Programme' was started in that year with a view to eliminate exploitation of the tribals by the money lenders, middlemen, prosperous and different farmers and the development of an institutional framework which would meet all their credit, consumer and produce marketing needs while formulating this programme, the socio-cultural environment of the tribals and the ecological imbalances have been taken into account.[8]

"During the Sixth Plan, a Modified Area Development Approach (MADA) was adopted to cover the smaller areas of tribal concentration, and during the Seventh Plan, the TSP strategy was extended further to cover even more smaller areas of tribal concentration and thus a cluster of tribal concentrations were identified.[9] 'The Eighth Plan had an overall objective of assisting 50 per cent of the total S.T. families below the poverty line to enable them to cross the poverty line. The Ninth Plan would aim to achieve the target of reducing the families below the poverty line in tune with the objectives."[10]

A major function of the Panchayati Raj is to formulate and to implement district and Panchayat Samiti's plan. Regarding the formulation of plans and programmes it is a well known fact that these are being formulated at the state and central levels. For long it was assumed that the socioeconomic environment acted equally upon people irrespective of their caste or social status. But the cultural environment, social values and legal systems were seemed to be biased in term of implementation of services rendered, such as land, credit facilities, education and training. The economic, political and other problems of the rural community had to be considered in the wider context of national and world politics and economy as well as of the policies of Central governments. The involvement of elected leaders in the planning process and implementation of development schemes is quite significant. The first priority would be to ensure perfect coordination between the people and Government and also to effectively implement the programmes focused on the betterment of the society, irrespective of caste, creed and religion, and take part in the welfare of the society. The initiative is a joint effort to find a peaceful solution to a problem that has affected the lives of the people.

If development programmes for tribals are to succeed, they must be clearly based on the tribals' clearly-expressed demands and priorities. The objective is to work at strengthening the existing human rights mechanism and develop practical action-oriented measures and strategies to combat intolerance. We would not be able to appropriately prepare ourselves for the future if our policies are not intrinsically linked to various events and, hence, we must be fully aware of what is happening. The Government has also been sensitive to the needs of SCs/STs and has formulated several policies and welfare programmes for the emancipation of SCs/STs (dalits) in the country through a large number of economic schemes. Our Constitution provides us firm guarantees of freedom, justice and democratic governance But there is a steep decline in moral values, corruption and ill-conceived ideologies which have paved the way to the failure of Government on all fronts on which our Constitution has stressed. Compromise of principles and ethical standards at all levels is widespread and all sections of people know about it. Corruption in the high places and unethical acts by politicians and Government officials have halted a person to live peacefully in society. It is a time to look back and examine where things went wrong, how and why. If not checked without delay, it could doubtlessly bring the entire system to a standstill and destroy the true meaning and essence of our noble Constitution.

The significance of all welfare schemes or programmes is only when such schemes or programmes are implemented or brought out of paper. Implementation depends upon the knowledge of programmes by the implementing agencies. Panchayati Raj institutions have been made the co-ordinating agencies for rural development activities, specially for implementing state and centrally sponsored schemes for the development and welfare of different sections of the rural society. Today, a maximum of the welfare programmes are implemented through PRIs. The involvement of elected leaders in the planning process and implementation of development schemes is quite significant. Educated people who realise the importance are not emotionally involved in the exercise. The decision will substantially ease the burden and provide people enough scope to ventilate their grievances and register their protests.

So the knowledge of welfare programmes by the members can be helpful in the implementation of the development programmes. Socioeconomic development can be boosted with the setting up of self-help groups (SHG) in rural areas and the participation of marginalised groups in development schemes. The members were asked: When did they have knowledge of the development programme?

Table 3.1

Knowledge of Programmes / Schemes

	Respondent		*Percentage*	
	Male	*Female*	*Male*	*Female*
Before getting membership	25	18	37.87	27.27
After getting membership	13	10	19.69	15.15

Out of the 66 members 43 had knowledge before becoming members and 23 got knowledge after getting to the post.

In the field survey, it was felt necessary to know from the elected members about the various development programmes being undertaken. All the 66 members including women seemed to be aware of the various programes; 45 members including 15 out of 28 women members had knowledge about Jawahar Rojgar Yojana (J.R.Y.); 49 members including 26 women had knowledge about Indira Awaz. Regarding old-age pension 63 out of 66 had knowledge. More men, i.e., 26, 21 and 20 out of 38 as compared to 8, 10 and 7 out of 28 women had knowledge about I.R.D.P., Balika Janam and Bank Khata respectively.

When questioned "What are these schemes?" all members except 5 to 6 Sarpanches, all Pradhans and Zila Pramukhs could not elaborate these schemes except old-age pension and Indira Awaz Yojna.

Implementation and Monitoring of Welfare Programmes and Schemes

There should be clear-cut definition of schemes and programmes that fall under the jurisdiction of PRIs. Change in national or state Government, the new Government is vowed to reverse the decision and policies in the name of rebuilding the national economy which surely hampers the acceleration of economic and development process. The Government must be sensitive to the needs of SCs/STs and should formulate policies and welfare programmes for the emancipation of SCs/STs (dalits) in the country through a large number of economic schemes. The Government should frame and implement policies and diversification programmes with a view to generate more and more employment opportunities. These efforts should be taken with multiple objectives of improving the employment avenues and improving state and national economy.

The plan process actually starts when the State Planning Department asks the Zila Parishads and Panchayat Samitis to formulate an annual plan for next year with restriction to the financial ceiling. This is then formulated as the district annual plan involving financial institutions including banks for providing financial assistance to the beneficiaries through their annual credit plan under social obligations.

Criteria for identifying the PR institution schemes and programmes could be as, firstly, schemes which can be planned and implemented at district and Panchayat Samiti levels, and secondly, schemes which can benefit the people living in the district and Panchayat Samiti concerned.

In our country the majority of people live, pursuing age-old traditional occupation like agriculture, which is a low-income generating job. With the majority of population settled in rural countryside the development programme should be aimed at generating income and employment to one and all. The implementation of policies in different

Table-3.2

Knowledge About Programmes / Schemes

	Respondent				*Percentage*			
	Male		*Female*		*Male*		*Female*	
	Having knowledge	*Having no knowledge*	*Having knowledge*	*Having no knowledge*	*Having knowledge*	*Having no knowledge*	*Having knowledge*	*Having no knowledge*
Jawahar Rozgar Yojana	30	8	15	13	45.45	12.12	22.72	19.69
Indira Awaz	23	15	26	2	34.84	22.72	39.39	3.03
I.R.D.P.	26	12	8	20	39.39	18.18	12.12	30.30
Old-Age Pension36	2	27	1	54.54	3.03	40.90	1.51	
Balika Janam	21	17	10	18	31.81	25.75	15.15	27.27
Bank Khata	20	18	7	21	30.30	27.27	10.60	31.81
Others	1	–	2	–	1.15	–	3.03	–

spheres—social, political, economic and scientific—will bring India to what was thought as apt in yester year by the architects of modern, secular and democratic India. Economic and political institutions of India must try to represent a picture of united India with all the constituents representing different religious, races, creeds and castes and should work shoulder to shoulder. What is needed is inspiration for the people to keep their ambitions, integrity of the nation and development coordinated. An attempt is made to analyse the implementation process and its effectiveness with reference to some schemes, which are administered by the Panchayat Samiti, which helps the people of the area to improve the standard of living. It is obvious that due to complete lack of organisation, supervision, monitoring, control and coordination of welfare schemes and programmes there is no improvement and development in economic and social conditions of the deprived sections. Most of these welfare schemes are being thwarted by bureaucratic apathy, and to remove this apathetic attitude a public official should be viewed as partners in the common task and not a hurdle in nation building. Timely and properly implemented programmes and schemes only could bring back smiles on the faces of deprived class. In this regard questions posed to the members were, "Have you applied or are you involved in these schemes? Or how do you educate or give knowledge to the people about the programmes and schemes?"

Table 3.3

Involvement in Programmes/Schemes

	Respondent		*Percentage*	
	Male	*Female*	*Male*	*Female*
Involved	15	8	22.72	12.12
Non-involved	23	20	34.84	30.30

Out of the 66 interviewed 23 responded positively whereas 43 told that they were not involved directly in the implementation of these schemes. About giving knowledge to the general people majority of a elected members responded that people are being informed through Gram Sabha and are also educated individually.

Entry as a Member

When asked about the influence that resulted in induction of them as members, they gave more than one reason that influenced them in getting to the post. Among 38 males, 17, 23, 11 and 22 had been influenced by their families, friends, community and organisation (political party) respectively. Among 28 women, 24, 17, 9 and 7 had the influence of family, friends, community and organisation (political party) respectively.

Table -3.4

Induction as Member

Influencing Factor	*Respondents*		*Percentage*	
	Male	*Female*	*Male*	*Female*
Family	17	24	25.75	36.36
Friend	23	17	34.84	25.75
Community	11	9	16.66	13.63
Teacher	3	–	4.54	–
Ideology	4	1	6.06	1.51
Institution	3	2	4.54	3.03
Organisation	22	7	33.33	10.60
Village	4	3	6.06	4.54
Others (Self/Life Partner)	5	1	7.57	1.51

It is observed that family and friends have the most impact in induction of men as well as women. Community has also some influence whereas organisations (political parties) have influenced more men than women. Only one woman out of 28 and five men out of 38 had decided on their own to enter politics. Education does not suggest any tangible effect of the determination of leadership, but age is found to be significant.

Attending Meetings and having Communications with People

Attending meeting is one of the most important variables of participation by which a member can listen to the views of general people and other elected members. In these meetings members can give suggestions and voice their grievances. They can be partners of the decision-making process and contribute to development. When it was asked whether they attended meetings regularly and what what their contribution, all members answered they attended meeting regularly.

It is very important to find out how many members address people in-groups and contact people individually because they are required to play a leadership role. Addressing in groups is the ability to communicate with the people and is an important channel of participation. Regarding giving knowledge to people, members were asked, how they educate people about welfare programmes.

Table 3.5

Knowledge of Programmes / Schemes given by Members to Local People

	Respondent		*Percentage*	
	Male	*Female*	*Male*	*Female*
By meeting individually	29	24	43.93	36.36
By meeting group-wise	38	26	57.57	39.39
Inactive role for giving knowledge	–	2	–	3.03

Among these, 38 male members answered that they communicated with people in groups whereas out of them 29 also met people individually. Out of 28 female members 2 had no contact with people, 2 contacted people only ingroups, whereas 24 had communication ingroups and also individually.

Views Regarding Education

Law cannot be self-applied and could help ensure equality

and justice only in a favourable atmosphere by awareness followed by educating each village and an individual but just how effective it will be is a moot question. Education is expected to serve as indicator of confidence in the strength and solidarity and bring in more development. Education is a mission that will be helpful in taking meaningful steps to establish coordination between procedures and timeframe implementation of measures, and would take care of all the woes.

It is an established fact that education is a thoughtful guide on how the governance can be improved, and how educated people themselves can play an important role in taking control of the rules that control their lives. Educating the people is a constructive attempt to find solutions, and empower ordinary citizens to use the right to information as lay the foundation for better decision making and communication.

We are satisfied with much less than our real potential. Education will help us believe in ourselves and approach everything with a whole heart and will always pull us through. Education is a tool for the people to understand their worth and potential so clearly that they will be inspired to see it in themselves. It will facilitate the way for helping people to optimise their capacities and potential, and allow them to fulfil their purpose and contribution for the benefit of both themselves and community. It plays a constructive role in participation virtues of an individual. It also helps in the development of human personality, social mobility, occupational change and the rise of professional, political and social awareness.

An educated person is more conscious of his rights as well as his duties, as a citizen of his country. Education increases the degree of participation, which is the key to development. It will enhance their ability to set goals for themselves and work in a planned way towards achieving their goals. These qualities will stand our country in good stead in the future. Education will help life continue at a reasonably normal pace. It will also help clear the cobwebs in people's mind and bring about a change in the mindset and the common perception. It will extol the virtues of grit, determination, hard work, perseverance, diligence which these are needed to pursue excellence with the highest degree of efficacy. We need to modify our education system to promote lateral thinking and innovation that will inevitably become tomorrow's reality. Once we set out to achieve all this, we can truly say that we are shaping the attitude of our people positively and giving them a push in the right direction.

Attitude is an inherent part of one's personality and has an impact on the people, working environment and family life. Education plays a decisive role in one's attitude, which is the mirror to one's mind and reflects one's thinking. It changes one's attitude to all about being proactive to the effect of bad incident because one cannot control what happens to one, but one can control one's attitude towards what happens to oneself. It is a catalyst in the positive thought process, which can be applied in day-to-day life.

Education can be used as the platform for human development and sharing of information on gender equality, campaigning against discrimination and advocating elimination of all sorts of discrimination. It is necessary to revive these in the rural areas where the girl education is neglected and where the SC/ST students are still backward. Mere participation cannot make an educational drive successful, concerted and collected team effort including women's participation is required. Efforts with the norms of human touch should also be made to ensure that the tempo is maintained in all times to come. With the increase and accessibility of schooling and provision of better facilities we can check the drop-out rate, and for this innovative programmes for education of girls and children belonging to the SC/ST should also be planned. These could pose serious problems if their performance is not up to the mark, so no laxity should be allowed to creep in at this crucial juncture. The time has come that people are taken into confidence and are provided with the best civic amenities, essential services and ample opportunity to avail of adequate resources which will set the stage for the massive development. It will create more opportunities to expand themselves and their personalities. It must be made compulsory for the state to take education seriously and not just a moral duty as is laid down in the Directive Principles of State Policy, and is after all a means of making wishes come true.

Since ancient time women have not been able to get their rightful place in society and their rightful place as citizens in the mainstream of society is ignored. They were considered incapable of knowing what was best for them. Education will play a major role in acquiring a certain "Know How" in the social life of women. It will serve as a means by which women can interpret/analyse the environment around them and also help in making rational decisions.

The strategic objective of women's education and human rights education may be explained as probing into the cause of deterioration in development of women empowerment and introduction of measures aimed at improving trust, cooperation and understanding between other sections of society (male). It also strengthens the existing human rights mechanism and develops practical action oriented measures and strategies to fight intolerance. Empowerment of women in robust sense of priorities should be taken as thought, a principle, a way of life, a movement. Everyone including women should be vowed to finish this as a mission to secure and rebuild the country and everyone should know this mission. There is some attention being paid by political parties and governments to the plight of women since last few years which is a welcome development. State and central governments have focused on reservation for women in educational institutions and jobs and introduced special schemes like the development of women and children in rural areas extending credit for self-employment schemes for groups of women and boosting their socio-economic development with setting up of self-help groups and their participation in development schemes.

Education will serve, as an indicator of confidence in women in giving strength and solidarity, and an extraordinary and exciting development that will speed up their abilities to develop solutions for challenges coming in their way. Education will help women in coordinating their activities with the others as much as possible, work for the people in the society and feel more connected to the rest of the population. Education will facilitate women in formation of self-help groups of women for their economic empowerment and will help in mobilising them to challenge the gender based social structure. It will also help in enabling them to recognise and exploit their potential, access government schemes and integrate the society.

Government and political parties must be steadfast in their commitment to India's ancient culture, democracy and way of life, and the convenience and rights of women should be respected. Women should have the same opportunity as men to fulfil their ambitions.

Instead of engaging themselves with the urgent political and socio-economic realities, our politicians and leaders use the suffering of people to step into the seat of power, and their mere aim is to retain power. We should look at various steps to check them and their subsequent consequences. It is believed that every bit of success has to be earned. This is the time to share the basic objectives and work in the same direction based on the objective because these days success depends on each other rather than solely on oneself. We must be prepared to change our behaviour till we get what we want. The success in the face of heavy odds will be an inspiration to all who dream of freedom, and would have a positive impact on the rest of the country. It should leave no one in doubt that economic reforms have created more possibilities of upward mobility. There have been times when we are involved in situations out of which there seems no way and this creates a general tendency to think on the negatives. We get into these situations not because we do things that are wrong, but because we approach our activities with divided intentions. We have to stop this scepticism, and what is important for us is to keep the improvement intact and focus on the positives. This will create more opportunities. If leaders study the entire scenario dispassionately they will visualise the substantial synergy.

Education plays an important role in every sphere of life and can play an important role in the development of a nation. It is also a matter of utmost significance not only for the upliftment of tribals and women but also for the general betterment of society. In all societies irrespective of whether they are tribal or highly civilised and modern, the chief aim of education is to impart knowledge. Education is the process of acquiring knowledge to live with dignity in a society and it is what makes possible the development of entire communities. It is important to provide the benefits of development and to put constitutional responsibilities above everything else. This has to be done to make it more representative by way of educating the masses, which will serve as an indicator of confidence in the strength and solidarity and bring in more development.

Tribal education is the constitutional obligation of both the state and central governments. The history of tribal and women education began with heated controversies about their right to education. Nobody should ignore the aspirations and yearning of people. All the parties must respect the desire of the people and take necessary step to resolve people's problems including human rights violations. Education is considered to be the key to modernisation and a catalyst to political and economic development of a society. It can quite simply be termed as an investment, that yields a higher profit than any other investment and education is equally important as employment.

There is clearly a lack of leadership in formulating an assessee programme to a poverty reduction strategy that will link education to improvement in the quality of life. Political power is normally in the hands of people having strong economic and social standing and these elites wielding economic power control politics and other social sub-systems to manipulate it to their own advantage. The political economy of education therefore is a dominating factor in determining education. People cannot afford to wait a long period of time for solutions. Government is trying to meet their expectations and change is in the air.

The purpose of the restructuring is to accelerate growth in education, which gives us flexibility to approach committed to the future growth strategy. Out of 66 members questioned 29 did not have formal education, that either they were illiterate or could only write their names. But it is very important that members must be aware about the importance of education in everyday life, whether they themselves are illiterate or they are educated. Education is a means and not an end in itself, and holds good for all levels and kinds of learning. The legislation could help ensure equality and justice only in a favourable atmosphere through awareness followed by education. Education has some connection with awareness of law. There is need to stem the tide through a tremendous amount of awareness building where a lot of issues like local governance and caste have to be factored in. Knowledge about the educational facilities is implied in participational process.

The student of rural society should also study the changing political modes of the rural people and the resultant increase of decline in the influence of different political parties among them. He should further investigate, by means of a sociological analysis, the causes that bring about the rise and fall of political parties in rural areas.

Table 3.6

Respondents' Opinion regarding Education

Opinion	*Respondents*		*Percentage*	
	Male	*Female*	*Male*	*Female*
No. of schools should be less	2	2	3.03	3.03
More (upgrade or anganwari)	4	5	6.06	7.57
New school should be open	12	3	18.18	4.54
Nos. are quite right	21	13	31.81	19.69
No comment	–	3	–	4.54
Others	10	2	15.15	3.03

The author asked about the educational facilities of the area, 34 out of 66 answered that the number of schools was all right, 15 said new schools should be opened and 12 said that schools should be upgraded. This shows that the majority of members are aware about the educational environment of their areas. Males were more aware about this because some of them told that existing schools were all right but upgrading them would be beneficial to the area.

When the author asked about the medium of education 56 out of 66 were of the opinion that Hindi should be the medium of teaching.

Health and Poverty

Nearly one-third of India's population has been considered to be below the 'poverty line', using certain criteria (Planning Commission 2001). Poverty does not only mean inadequate access to food but also deprivation of several basic requirements for healthy life. Thus poverty implies poor environment and self-reliance and poor access to health care.

Emergency and hospitalisation services are almost non-existent in the government-run health care programmes in the rural area. Since the majority of the population (70 per cent) lives in the rural areas, rural health needs to be the focus of the state policy. The Government of India in 1985 in the chapter of health and family welfare of the seventh five-year plan stated health as the key variable and prerequisite for human resource development. A person is entitled to the right to life, and human life is of paramount importance. So providing medical facilities to its people is the prime duty of government. Health services in rural areas, especially tribal areas with adequate staff and required drugs are very much essential. Tribal women's health has to be improved not only to ensure better health and survival of their children and reduction of population growth rates but also for tribal women themselves and for improving the overall health status of the society. Till now, tribal women's health has been viewed from the prospective of maternal health through immunisation and family planning programmes.

Government, while providing medical facilities to the rural and tribal population, gives more stress to family planning, ignoring the health sector of the population. So the population has to depend upon the private and expensive medical facilities, which is a burden on the rural and tribal populations. The persistent poverty and disease syndromes have pushed the tribal families away from the mainstream. There is need to reassert a public health perspective in economy and social services. The people are not only deprived of basic health services but also other basic needs like proper food and drinking water. Food intake and levels of nutrition have been found to be important and accurate proxies of income distribution. At the panchayat level there is a need to integrate health, water supply and government agencies including panchayati raj departments to bring an effective public health policy and a responsive health services.

Due to geographical conditions of T.S.P. (Tribal Sub Plan) area it is very difficult for the people to get medical facilities, due to lack of inadequate infrastuctural facilities. It is also difficult for the medical staff to provide medical facilities. According to the 1991 census, health facility is available 5-10 kms, far from the villages. Moreover, the norms prescribed for primary health centres and sub-centres for other areas are not very much appropriate in the tribal regions because of the hilly terrain, inaccessible areas and dispersal of population in small settlements over a large area. The tribals have little or no access even to the most elementary form of health care, and do not enjoy even the basic health facilities.

The health status or sickness of a community, especially within a modern nation state, is required to be understood to siut the social conditions. The social conditions include access to the basic needs and amenities like food, drinking water, housing, education, employment, transport, communication, etc. Improvement in basic health services has to be accorded with high priority in any development programme meant for the rural and tribal community

Availability of transportation in a particular region shows the infrastructural development. It is often seen in tribal regions that due to the typical topography, the status of road is kaccha and the Sagwara Panchayat Samiti, which is in Dungarpur District, Rajasthan State, is also no exception to it. During the visit I met Mrs. Jeewanda Devi, she is A.N.M. Her dispensary is at Kahela Panchayat in Dungarpur District, which is connected by a kacca road. She is a very dedicated lady. She always attends the M.S.S. meetings and gives knowledge to pregnant women. But her main problem is that patients cannot reach in time due to the katcca road and no transportation facility is available to them. She attends her patients on her husband's motor-cycle sometimes it becomes very late.

The present poverty and disease syndromes have put the tribals into debt to meet their day-to-day needs of health care. They are forced to spend a major proportion of their income on health care. Many people have had to sell their land and property to undergo treatment. A majority of tribal population resides in backward, hilly and remote regions where health facilities, may it be government or private, are not available. They have to depend heavily upon faith healers and poor quality health service provided by unqualified local practitioners. "The tribal people living closest to nature are influenced more by socio-cultural and environmental dimensions in their healing practices. Tribal health-care systems are based on herbal medicines, ayurvedic medicines and other related systems like sidha and yoga rituals, along with a strong leaning towards magico-religious practices associated with appeasement of God and keeping the evil spirits at bay".[11]

Problems of health and hygiene have a direct bearing on the economic and demographic aspects of the tribes. Access to health care requires the availability and affordability of the medical facilities. There is thus a strong link between poverty, deprivation and ill-health. "Poverty is a social and political phenomenon as much as an economic problem and thus requires political and social changes, particularly within the site of power."[12] Poverty is the economic consequence of social backwardness and political deprivation. "Economic conditions determine the social status of an individual or group of individuals".[13] Participation in local administration will be helpful in enabling people below the poverty line to express and analyse the realities of their social status and economic inadequacy, evaluate by themselves their actions in furtherance of their objectives. Each person is the best judge of his circumstances and hence, he must be given an opportunity to participate in all matters concerning alleviation and elimination of the difficulties in which he is placed, such as poverty.

Low nutrition standards, low health standards and a low-income level undermine people's self-help capacities and reduce their efforts in participation in decision-making procedures and implementation of development programmes. A large section of the tribal and rural population of the country lives under conditions of acute poverty. Before they can envisage the democratic possibility of their being able to actively participate in decision-making process influencing the politico-economic and socio-cultural affairs of the republic, one has to think of their minimal needs, education health care and so on.[14] Improvement in the health status of the population has been one of the major thrust areas in social development programmes of the country. This was to be achieved through improving the access to and utilisation of health, family welfare and nutrition services with special focus on under-served and under-privileged segments of the population.[15]

The accessibility and availability of government health services varies from areas near to urban dwelling and remote in term of distribution of institution, availability of manpower and related infrastructure.

Primary health care (PHC) is the backbone of the health delivery system in each state. In the report, Financing Primary Health Care in Andhra Pradesh, prepared for World Health Organisation 1997 by K. Sujatha Rao, she clearly states that PHCs do not adequate facilities to provide health services effectively, and utilisation of these facilities is very low. It is mandatory on the part of each state government to expand and upgrade its facilities to meet the growing health care requirements in rural and tribal areas.

Mass-media Exposure

The transfer of information from one individual or group to another, whether in speech or through the mass media of modern times is crucial to any society.[16] Communication problems were still evident between elected Scheduled Caste/ Scheduled Tribe Panchayat members, other Panchayat members and government officials. In some cases Scheduled Castes and Scheduled Tribes seemed to lack exposure to other communities in a context other than being a servant or a labourer.[17]

Table 3.7

Knowledge about the Names of Newspapers

	Respondents		*Percentage*	
	Male	*Female*	*Male*	*Female*
Having knowledge	15	8	22.72	12.12
Having no knowledge	23	20	34.84	30.30

"Communication makes human social life possible. The nature and quality of our communication process mould the character of our social life."[18] The central idea of democracy is that ordinary citizens should control what their government does. Mass media commands a great influence in political, social and educational fields and can play a vital role in awareness generation. The media plays a central role in the development of modern institutions, and communication is considered as an important component of modernisation. It increases the knowledge and awareness of an individual, broadens his outlook and helps him in getting rid of parochial values and beliefs. It would motivate him to be actively involved in the democratic process and to increase his efficiency. It makes people fully aware of what is happening, otherwise they would not be able to appropriately prepare themselves for the future.

The transfer of information from one individual or group to another, whether in speech or through the mass media of modern-time is crucial in any society.[19] The mass media are often associated only with entertainment and, as such, are seen as rather marginal to most people's lives. Such a view is a partial one. However, mass communication is involved in many other aspects of our social activities too. Media like newspapers or television have a wide-ranging influence over our experience and over public opinions. This is not just because they affect our attitudes in specific ways, but because they are the means of access to the knowledge on which many social activities depend.

"Mass communication has become today a means of various types of knowledge. Without it we can miss the up-to-date knowledge of the modern world."[20] Face-to-face interaction, such as people talking at a party, is rich in clues used by individuals to make sense of what others say. Mediated interaction involves the use of media technology—paper, electrical connections, electronic impulses. A characteristic of mediated interaction is that it is stretched out in time and space; it goes well beyond the contexts of ordinary face-to-face interaction. A third type of interaction is mediated quasi-interaction. This refers to the sort of social relations created by the mass media. Such interaction is stretched across time and space, but it doesn't link individuals directly: hence the term 'quasi-interaction'.[21]

One role of media in democracy is that of being a watchdog over government. Citizens can hold officials accountable for setting things right only if they know about errors and wrongdoings. Walter Lapmann once declared that "a free press is not a privilege but an organic necessity in a great society. Without criticism and reliable and intelligent reporting, the government cannot govern." (Walter Lapmann, address in London on, May 27, 1965.) Most of the information must come through the mass media. How well elected members work depends partly on how good a job the mass media are doing.

A second role of mass media is to make clear what the political parties stand for and how the candidates shape up in term of personal character, knowledge, experience, and position on the issues. Without such information, it is difficult for voters to make intelligent choices.

A third role of mass media is to present a diverse, full and enlightening set of facts and ideas about public policy. The mass media clearly play important parts in the political system. They act as amplifiers for speaking to citizens and trying to persuade them. The media also serve as channels of communication among political and governmental institutions.

Tribals have been living in isolation for centuries past. The main reason for this isolation is lack of communication. Development of communication no doubt will provide greater opportunities for the tribal folk to develop national consciousness and a healthier intellectual horizon.[22] In many ways, mass communication has progressed and improved more than any other aspect of modern living. Its impact, therefore, has been vastly increased and is now dominant in determining what course events shall take.

Channel of Communication

Roads are the most important means of communication as far as the population living in remote areas is concerned. The media have changed more rapidly. Radio significantly changed the face of the mass media. Newspapers have been joined as sources of political news by increasing numbers of magazines; then by radio and television and most recently, by new, interactive media like the internet, which permit instant communication among citizens and public officials. Modern communications technology, including e-mail and the fax, has made it possible for an even more rapid turn around time.

A large number of rural people are illiterate, ignorant and poorly informed about ongoing issues, debates and reforms concerning the society in general and women in particular. Communication can be direct or indirect, face-to-face contact of the impersonal channel. Mass media can play a vital role in awareness generation and help in building up innovative personality.

The means of communication for mobilising local resources and to solve problems affecting remotely settled population, have wide a range covering local and national newspaper, posters, local radios loudspeaker, pamphlets, slides, taperecorders, exhibition, local fairs, films, music and puppet shows, and *nautankees*. Women can be motivated and inspired to think, discuss and act politically with the help of documentaries, television and radio. Education is now more important to more people, and today the major media are the institutions. You may be able to influence such formal means of internal communication at staff meetings. You may be able to influence such informal communication channel as conversation exchanges between individuals.

Migration and Urban Exposure

The tribals of the area are either landless or marginal cultivators. Even the land possessed by them is either infertile or lacks irrigation facility. As a result tribals hardly manage livelihood by agriculture. Acute and persistent poverty is one of the basic problems afflicting our country. The dimension of rural poverty in India is varied and is linked with unemployment, under-employment, low level of productivity, severe demographic pressure and illiteracy. As both tribal men and women are equally responsible for family earnings, they migrate to nearby urban settings for search of work. So the contractors and other persons begin them to exploit as cheap labour. Special efforts in the planning process will have to be directed towards ameliorating the depressed social and economic conditions of those who fall below the poverty line. Unless education, income, employment and political activities are not stimulated, these would have implications for achieving the required growth of rural poor. Education and knowledge secure for the purpose the much-coveted freedom from the miseries of life. "Migration of people may be considered as an instrument of cultural diffusion and social integration that results into more meaningful distribution of population."[23]

Migration is one of the factors of urban population growth. Growth of population in urban areas is not only due to a fall in death rate or increase in the birth rate but also due to rapid migration to these areas from rural areas. It is imperative on the part of the government and its agencies to provide better focus and direction of programmes and schemes in bringing about sustained improvement in the economic conditions of the rural poor.

Participation of people can be encouraged through beneficiaries / functional committees which should be given the responsibility of overseeing the implementation of various programmes. This will go a long way in avoiding some of the pitfalls that plague our planning with disastrous consequences. The government machinery, voluntary organisations and self-help groups should be involved in the process of advocacy and in organising the people, especially the poor. This can be achieved by involving the people right from the lowest levels not only in the implementation but also in the formulation of plans. Migration is much influenced by the attainment of literacy, particularly functional literacy. Training, technology extension and skill upgradation of the people and leaders in urban and rural set-up by central and state agencies are the subjects of vital necessity in our country for sustainable development.

Reservation

Reservation is a tool of participation in political process and can be effective in the national development process. We need several systemic changes, which should aim at empowering the individual in India. "In rural India, traditionally leadership positions were secured by persons belonging to higher castes with better economic conditions."[24] "Constitution provides for affirmative action by way of reservation so as to provide impetus to certain class of persons, who are not able to reach the desired level of participation in public life and suffer from handicap of social and educational backwardness, and who require positive discrimination in their favour.

Today tribals enjoy a formally and explicitly recognised right to education, but specific and effective government policies have ensured that their access to education is secured. Their population, social and educational standard and status have undergone a drastic change as earlier they were deprived of education and civilised life and they suffered from backwardness, illiteracy and poverty. The best possible start in life for children is to have access to quality basic education, including free and compulsory primary education, and ample opportunity for children and adolescents to develop their individual capacities. State governments should implement programmes relating to all areas of child development. People who are chosen usually don't have the skills, the orientation or the aspiration to understand when things go wrong. The key factor is that they have the responsibility but not the authority. They can suffer from lack of recognition for the key role they play. They must be able to communicate.

The most basic job is taking care of all the day-to-day problems. Our experience has shown that a multidimensional approach towards family and community betterment with emphasis on education, skill development, income generation and women's development works more effectively than laws as rightly said by Earl Warren, "It is the spirit and not the form of law that keeps justice alive." It is only the beginning, so let's wait, not watch. This comes from a sense of belonging to one's surroundings, an involvement with one's people. Politically aware everyone has an opinion. Sometimes they can be too opinionated and even the grassroots got involved. But it is very essential to study the impact of reservation on the social life of tribals while studying the impact of reservation on their political right. When a tribal is elected to any political body, he aquires statutory status and also gains some power. He has a part to improve but most people suffer, generally from poor lifestyle habits and lack of activity that is heavily influenced by society. Every now and then a person may find himself facing a challenge moving through life transition. We must first understand how structural, political linkage, and government factors shape interest groups and what they do. Reservation then becomes one form of increasing political participation in the sphere of representative institutions. A step towards achieving perfection is to develop an awareness about how he feels about himself. How he is treated socially is a subject of concern.

Table 3.8

Reaction towards Reservation Policy

		Respondents		*Percentage*	
		Male	*Female*	*Male*	*Female*
Social tension	Yes	14	4	21.21	6.06
	No	22	19	33.33	28.78
Benefits to adivasis	Yes	33	22	50.00	33.33
	No	3	2	4.54	3.03
Mental development of adivasis	Yes	34	24	51.51	36.36
	No	2	-	3.03	-
Deterioration Administrative level	Yes	3	1	4.54	1.51
	No	11	4	16.66	6.06
No comment		2	4	3.03	6.06

Forty-one out of 66 were of the opinion that there was no tension, their population, social and educational standard and status had undergone a drastic change; 18 were of the opinion that reservation had brought tension among tribals and general population who were deprived of education and civilised life and they suffered from backwardness, illiteracy and poverty; six did not give any comment. When asked whether any tribals benefited by the reservation, 55 out of 66 said that tribals were benefited by reservation policy, five were of the opinion that tribals were not benefited and six gave no opinion. Again asked about the effect of reservation on mental development of Adivasis, 58 were of the opinion that reservation had changed their mental level through reservation in education, politics and services in order to accelerate economic growth. It should leave no one in doubt that reservation has created more responsibilities of upward spectrum and this has drawn sustenance from the country's pluralistic cultural traditions.

The respective governments must pay serious attention to fine-tuning proactive policies. Two were of the opinion that there was no change in their mental level whereas six had no opinion. When asked about the standard of administration after the reservation, 15 answered that there was no fall in administrative level; four said there was a fall in administrative level because they had the responsibility but not the authority, 47 were not aware about the administrative standard.

Table 3.9
Tribals' Relations with General People (After Independence)

	Respondents		*Percentage*	
	Male	*Female*	*Male*	*Female*
Better	2	–	3.03	–
Good	10	9	15.15	13.63
Normal	22	19	33.33	28.78
Worse	4	–	6.06	–

Another question was whether relation with general people had changed since Independence; 21 were of the opinion that general people (high-caste) were very polite towards them; 41 said that the attitude of the general people had changed and relation with them was normal; four said that relationship between tribals and general people deteriorated.

Reasons and Remedies for Tribals Inequality

There is a hypothesis that reservation and other steps taken by the central and state governments have brought equality and justice to the tribals.

When enquired about the reasons which are responsible for the inequality of tribals, there were various answers; 58 out of 66 members said that absence of unity among the tribals was the main reason as they were divided in many groups and were quarrelling among themselves for supremacy instead of fighting for their rights. Education brought changes in mental level of any person. So was the case of the tribals of Rajasthan whereas the tribals of many states were enjoying the fruits of equality in Rajasthan they were being exploited. The range of activities was very wide and the provision of reservations had not led to tribal participating in decision making in social bodies; 57 out of 66 felt that lack of education led to increased dejected attitude of tribals, which was one of the main reasons for inequality of tribals; 32 out of 66 felt that biased attitude of government officials, nowadays considered tribals as commodity to be exploited, was another reson; 29 out of 66 fell that use of tribals as vote bank by the political parties and the indifferent attitude of government and political parties had not brought the equal status of tribals as sought by the framers of the Constitution; 22 out of 66 felt that the unwillingness of government in implementing of policies had not brought the position of tribals to the expected level; 15 out of 66 thought that a shortfall in the implementation of policies and not making implementing agencies responsible and accountable were responsible for not giving the tribals the status which they deserved.

Table 3.10

Reasons of Social Inequality

	Respondents		*Percentage*	
	Male	*Female*	*Male*	*Female*
Short fall in low implementation	10	5	15.15	7.57
Unfavourable attitude of govt. & political parties.	21	8	31.81	12.12
Unwillingness of govt., in implementing policies	9	13	13.63	19.69
Biased Govt. officials	19	13	28.78	19.69
Absence of unity among tribals	34	24	51.51	36.36
Dejected attitude of tribals	33	24	50.00	36.36
No comments	–	2		

It is observed in our enquiry that there are many reasons, which are responsible for the tribals' status, which is not to the standard, as they deserve. A question was, how can inequality of tribals be minimised?

Table 3.11

Opinion to Strengthen the Tribals

Variables for Strengthening	*Respondents*		*Percentage*	
	Male	*Female*	*Male*	*Female*
Education	18	6	27.27	9.09
Employment	5	3	7.57	4.54
Collectiveness among tribal	23	20	34.84	30.30
Role of government	19	10	28.78	15.15
Role of political party	6	8	9.09	12.12
No comment	1	1	1.51	1.51

Forty-three out of 66 told that collectiveness among tribals could be an effective tool for bringing the tribals to the equal status and strengthen them; 29 out of 66 felt that government must not limit itself up to framing of law and policies for the welfare of the tribals but it should change its role in implementing them by bringing in a legislature, which can make the implementing agencies accountable under law. Political parties should change their indifferent attitude towards tribals as being their vote bank only; they must their keep promises of election. This was the opinion of 15 out of 66 members.

Making policies and welfare schemes are fruitless because tribals are not educated. Infrastructure for education should be up to the mark that will provide education to tribals and this can bring changes and strengthen them. This was the opinion of 24 out of 66 members. Tribals being agriculturists by profession in remote dwellings, only eight out of 66 felt that employment could strengthen them.

Role of Political Parties

Political parties are responsible for bringing a general political awakening among the masses. They are the most important unit of political set-up in democratic countries. They are a medium of struggle for power; at the same time it is an agency to give political education to the people. In the area under study political parties have very few activities. They are a feature of the parliamentary system of government, which has been adopted in India. At the national or state level in India it is difficult, rather impossible, to achieve political position without being an affiliation to any political party. But for achieving political power at the village level and for attaining position in village panchayat it is debatable that affiliation with political parties is necessary or even desirable. The role of parties in village politics assumes particular importance in the context of Panchayati Raj. The effectiveness of political parties depend upon the participation of masses in politics. A party's activities at the local level are often controlled by people who do not have clear ideas about the principles for which their leaders stand at the all-India level. Out of the total respondents only 77.27 per cent respondents are members of political parties. The vagueness of party membership is a good indicator of the ambiguous nature of our parties. Election provides an opportunity for participating in the general political process. It not only involves the casting of votes but also gives chances for attending election meetings, pamphleteering and using various propaganda materials. "At the Gram Panchayat level, political parties provided some promising candidates with little party support in cash and kind. However, political affiliations were less pronounced and parties did not carry out an elaborated election campaign."[25]

It is very essential to study the various political parties operating in the rural areas. These parties express the specific interest and aspirations of various classes and socio-economic groups composed of rural people such as landlords, tenants, land-labourers, peasants, proprietors and others. They voice their desire and determination to secure political power and use it to modify or overhaul the existing social system in consonance with their own interests and social objectives. Politicians' ambitions force them to anticipate what the public wants and to accomplish it. The political parties make promises, but when it comes to implementing these promises, the parties take a different path. People cannot afford to wait a long period of time for a solution. The impact of political parties happens to be very less in a rural society.

It has been seen that villagers usually do not take active part in the higher level politics an, i.e., assembly and parliamentary elections in rural areas is poor. In the election of village panchayat it has generally been observed that elections are fought on individual basis and not on the party basis. The Indian rural community in general is very much detached from the activities of the political parties in India. In a democratic country political parties obviously play a vital role. The level of political consciousness promoted by the political education programme of the party inspires political action, which throws up new political leaders. The process of building up leadership, the channelisation of struggle for power and the political education for masses all go hand in hand with the political parties. The propaganda of political parties do not reach the villagers to acquaint them about the principles, ideologies, or personalities of the political parties. This is one of the reasons that active membership or working of political parties in rural areas and especially in tribal areas is very significant.

Government is trying to meet their expectations and change is in the air. The purpose of the restructuring is to accelerate growth in education. The party system provides the channel between government and the masses in a democratic set-up. Political parties are organisations that try to win control of government by getting elected to public office by people who carry the party label. Obviously, parties want to win election and put their people in office. But for what purpose? That question is not easy to answer, given the fragmentation and complexity of the party organisation. Political parties are entirely devoid of tools to encourage coordination and cooperation among their various levels. Each party component tends to have its own goals.

Campaign against the mass illiteracy among the rural people is the urgent task today. Further, treasures of rich modern knowledge have to be brought within their reach if they are to be effective participants in the creative work of national reconstruction. The problem of teaching and directing personnel is another baffling problem. The literacy is particularly necessary in the village today, because, due to its absence, a large number of even those few who have become literate through elementary village school education cannot maintain their ability to read, and hence lapse into illiteracy. "Political parties can do a number of things to make popular sovereignty possible, such as keeping elected officials responsive and responsible, incorporating a wide range of groups into politics, heightening political interest among the public, and ensuring accountability."[26]

Political parties are essential to democracy and can be tools of popular sovereignty. Parties are not only organisations and office holders but also images in the minds of voters and potential voters, mental cues that affect the behaviour of the electorate. The government activity is only one aspect of the political life of the village population. Non-governmental political organisations also have emerged and are functioning in the rural area in modern times. Nobody should ignore the aspirations of the people. All the parties must respect the desire of the people and necessary step to resolve peoples' problems including human rights, violations. Political parties can provide a way for the people to keep elected officials responsive through competitive elections. Political parties are also important for popular sovereignty because they generally try to include as many groups in the population as they possibly can.

Weaker political parties are not good for democracy. Weaker parties also mean that interest groups have greater access to political decisionmakers. Without strong parties, politics become more volatile, interest groups become more influential, and public policy becomes less coherent. It is difficult for the parties to provide governance that is coherent, consistent, and effective.

Views regarding Women

It is an assumption that the socio-economic environment acted equally upon people irrespective of their sex status. Elizabeth Cady Stanton stated that "all men and women are created equal, endowed with the same inalienable rights." In reality, the status of women is very different from men. Even as the victim of the gender discrimination of our social system, women have been forced to be subordinate to their male counterpart and have failed to develop themselves as important ingredient of political system. The process of women empowerment is required for breaking away the cycle of learned and taught submission to discrimination, carried on from one generation of women to the next.

Independence of India has opened the doors for women of the country to get their due recognition from the society and partake in the political, social and administrative life of the country. The future of development of the society lies in the future of women equally with men. The behaviour of women strongly dependent on the situation, without the reservation quota they would not compete for panchayat. All political parties have committed themselves to reservation for women in their struggle for gender equality. "Politicians' ambitions force them to anticipate in what the public wants and to accomplish it."[27] But the hollowness of their commitment is clearly exposed, in fact, that they have never allowed women to participate in decision making within their own party structure. The presence and participation of women is woefully inadequate at all panchayats. The mental set-up of the male population in rural areas has to undergo a change to facilitate acceptance of women as chairpersons of Panchayats. "The 'participation of women' is difficult to assess, because the involvement of women in decision-making procedures largely depends on the kind of the reserved seats in the Panchayats (chairperson's seats or ordinary seats). If provided with opportunities women may or may not participate, but without adequate opportunities women do not struggle for participation."[28] "The reservation, in particular the reservation for chairpersons, provide women with a tremendous opportunity to partake in village, block and district level politics which they would otherwise not have obtained."[29]

The 73rd Amendment constitutes the PRIs as self-governing institutions, and as the third tier in the federal structure of India. So it was duty of the researcher to find out their status and participational quality in PRI's to the powers delegated by government through the 73rd amendment. Earlier we have taken into account their inclusion as member, attending meetings and also their opinion on many important issues. But it is essential to find out how far have they reached in bearing responsibility and what are the drawbacks?

Table 3.12

Role of Women Members towards Responsibility

	Respondents		*Percentage*	
	Male	*Female*	*Male*	*Female*
Able to bear their responsibility	25	28	37.87	42.42
Unable to bear their responsibility	13	–	19.69	–
Reasons for inability to bear their responsibility				
1. Lack of education	7	–	10.60	–
2. Dependency	4	–	6.06	–
3. Lack of self -decision	2	–	3.03	–

A question was asked to the elected members interviewed about women's capability of bearing responsibility. This was the general observation in our field study—if provided with opportunities women may or may not participate, but without adequate opportunities women do not struggle for participate; 25 out of 38 male members said that women members are capable of bearing responsibility and all female members were of the opinion that women are capable of bearing responsibility. When asked from the members with negative response that is the reason behind women not bearing responsibility; seven out of 13 pointed out lack of education, four were of the opinion that their dependency on others were and lack of self decision as the drawback.

When asked to give suggestions for better performance of female members in bearing responsibility towards PRI's there were many suggestions—32 out of 38 male members suggested education as the catalyst in the performance of women members, and 12 out of 28 women members were of the same opinion; 16 out of 28 said self-decision and self-confidence were the causes in the performance of female members and eight out of 28 females were with their male counterpart.

Table 3.13

Respondents' Suggestions to Women Members

Variables of suggestion	*Respondents*		*Percentage*	
	Male	*Female*	*Male*	*Female*
Education	32	12	48.48	18.18
Health	7	5	10.60	7.57
Group discussion	4	1	6.06	1.51
Employment	3	–	4.54	–
Self confidence & self-decision	16	8	24.24	12.12
Having no suggestions	3	4	4.54	6.06

Health plays an important role in participation, tribal women's health has to be improved not only to ensure better health and survival of their children and reduction of population growth rates but also for tribal women themselves and for improving the overall health status of the society. Till now, tribal women's health has been viewed from the perspective of maternal health through immunisation and family planning programmes but it should be viewed keeping in mind their performance and involvement in political process. Seven out of 38 males and five out of 28 females said that sound health would help women in better performance. Group discussion and employment were other factors affecting the performance of women in PRI's. Seven out of 66 could not give any suggestions. The "Participation of Women" is difficult to assess, because the involvement of women in decision-making procedures largely depends on education but it is accepted that the status of women has a direct relationship with the level of development of society. Women elected members have to be made fully conscious of their rights and responsibilities.

Training Programme and Camps

The elected repres entatives of the people, whether men or women would require to be trained to enable them to discharge their functions in an effective manner. The success or failure of Panchayati Raj—the political order based on Panchayats—depends to a large extent on the preparedness of the Indian village to utilise in democratic ways the wider powers being given to it. There is a need for comprehensive and meaningful training programme for rural women for performing their constitutional duties and responsibilities as members of PRIs. The government was taking steps towards restructuring training and carrying out capacity-building programmes to face the emerging challenges

Employment and Income

Closely associated with the problem of poverty is the problem of unemployment. Though unemployment is universal yet in India it is more marked. Employment that can be termed as human capital is the key factor and important investment in the development process. "Poverty and exploitation are now synonymous with the majority of tribal population."[30] "Unemployment means a wastage of manpower and productive effort."[31] Lack of education, unhealthy condition of the rural areas, too much growth of population have worsened the economic life of the rural people. The economic prosperity and development of a region depends much on the network of transport and communications. A radically new strategy is needed for eradicating unemployment and improving the living conditions of millions of Indians. In reducing the inequality, the solution lies in the fact that the wage earners, small landowners and unemployed youth should be persuaded to attend adult classes in a massive way. Women employment paves the way for women's integration in the process of national development.

Political Activities

Local government is a significant and vital institution in the framework of our society. The government machinery, voluntary organisations and self-help groups should be involved in the process of advocacy and in organising the people, especially the poor. This can be achieved by involving people right from the lowest levels not only in the implementation but also in the formulation of plans. Elections to local bodies have given a new impetus for the functioning of development institutions at the grassroots level. Gram Sabha is established for forwarding peoples' demands, grievances, complaints, needs, etc., to the government for a solution. The meeting of a Gram Panchayat should be public and should be held at a public place. Members have to take oath of allegiance as usual. They have to attend meetings regularly. Every member is also liable for the loss, waste and misappropriation of any money or property belonging to the Panchayat. The Gram Sabha should list out priorities and assist in the selection of beneficiaries for various programmes and schemes. In this way, the aspirations of the people would be articulated. The Gram Sabha is also to assist the Gram Panchayat in its activities and mobilisation of local resources. It is expected to promote social harmony and social awareness among the people. Political participation is political activity by individuals.

With regard to people's participation in the planning process it was found that women are actively involved in the planning process, and they attend meetings of the Gram Sabha.

Table 3.14: Attending the Gram Sabha

	Respondent		*Percentage*	
	Male	*Female*	*Male*	*Female*
Attended	25	16	37.88	24.24
Not attended	13	12	19.70	18.18

Participation does not exist in the abstract, but is defined through the individuals involved, specific institutions, processes and ideological and cultural factors. Within any participatory structure, overall forms of social inequality and oppression are usually reflected and maintained. The role of Gram Sabha regarding the supervision and control over Gram Panchayat is ineffective, and the attitude of the villagers towards this body is quite insufficient. The meetings of Gram Sabha are either not held or are poorly attended by rural people, specially women. "The indicator 'Political Awareness and Participation' refers to the political involvement and the political awareness of Panchayat members, and the electorate of the village community (Gram Sabha). It should be taken into consideration that political participation in a hierarchically stratified society often depends more upon opportunities made available by higher level politicians than on the individual commitment or the skills of the Panchayat members."[32] It is a small government approach which reduces the massive structure of the government and increases the responsibilities of the people. Government is not a provider but a facilitator for the people to take initiative to bring development, equity and social justice. The people and the leaders should know their responsibilities.

REFERENCES

1. Edward S. Greenberg & Benjamin I. Page, *The Struggle for Democracy,* Wesley Educational Publishers Inc. United States, 1999, p.10.
2. Weber Max, *The Theory of Social and Economic Organisation,* Oxford University Press, New York, 1947, p.147.
3. Manoj Sharma, *Rajasthan Vikas,* April-July, 2001, p.8.
4. F.W.Riggs, *Bureaucracy and Political Development*, Princeton, N. Univ. Press, 1963, p.139.
5. Samuel P. Huntington, Political Development and Political Decay, *World Politics*, Vol. XVIII, No.3, April 1963, p.388.
6. Uphoff, N.T. and Cohen, J., *Feasibility and Application of Rural Development Participation: A State of the Art Paper,* Cornell University, U.S.A., 1979.
7. Sixth Five Year Plan, *Government of India,* Planning Commission, 1980-85, p.418.
8. *Draft Sixth Five Year Tribal Sub Plan Area: Rajasthan, 1980-85*, Tribal Area Development Department, Rajasthan, Udaipur, p.1.
9. Tribal Development Project: A Glance, September 1999, Government of India, Ministry of Social Justice And Empowerment Tribal Development Division, New Delhi, p. (i)

10. *Ninth Five-Year Plan for Tribal Development: in Rajasthan,* Volume I, *1997-2002, Including Annual Plan 1997-1998.*
11. Bhupendra Singh, Neeti Mohanti (eds.), *Tribal Health in India,* Inter India Publications, New Delhi, 1995, p.50.
12. Ashine Roy, *Human Rights of Women*, Rajat Publications, New Delhi, 2003, p.219.
13. George Dalton, *Economic Development and Social Change,* Basic Book Inc. Publishers, New York, pp. 269-294.
14. Berthold Kuhn, *Participatory Development in Rural India,* Radiant Publishers, New Delhi, 1998, p.52.
15. Government of India, Planning Commission, *Approach Paper to the Tenth Five-Year Plan* (2002-2007), New Delhi, September 2001.
16. Karen Birdsall, *Sociology*, Polity Press, U.K., 2000, p.46.
17. Berthold Kuhn, op. cit., p.225.
18. Paul B. Horton, Gerald R. Leslie, *The Sociology of Social Problems*, Printice-Hall, Inc., United States of America, 1978, p.482.
19. Anthony Giddens, *Sociology,* Polity Press, Cambridge, U.K., 2002.
20. Arti Mishra, *Women in Slums: Impact of Environmental Pollution,* Classing Publishing Company, New Delhi, 2004.
21. Karen Birdsall, op. cit., p.463.
22. Nadeem Husnain, *Tribal India,* Palka Prakashan, Delhi, 1999.
23. Sudeepta Adhikari, *Political Geography,* Rawat Publication, Jaipur, 1997, p. 298.
24. Iqbal Narain, *The Rural Elite in an Indian State—A Case Study of Rajasthan,* Manohar Book Depot, New Delhi, 1976, p.72.
25. Berthold Kuhn, op. cit., p.259.
26. A. James Richley, *The Life of the Parties: A History of American Political Parties,* Free Press, New York, 1992.
27. Moris P. Fiorina, *Retrospective Voting in American National Elections*, M A: Harvard University Press, Cambridge, 1981.
28. Berthold Kuhn, op. cit., p.117.
29. Ibid., p. 271.
30. Nadeem Husain, op. cit., p.183.
31. Lucy Mair, *An Introduction to Social Anthropology,* Oxford University Press, London, 1972, p.181.
32. Berthold Kuhn, *op. cit.*, p.117.

4

Performance of Women as Members

Socio-political Background of the Elected Women Members

Women's development is directly related to national development. In the sixth five year plan a special chapter has been added 'Women Development'. In this it has been mentioned that the strategy should be threefold, i.e., education, employment and health. They are interdependent and dependent on the total development process. The socio-economic background of the individuals is a relevant variable in the understanding of his place in the social structure.[1] "The biological division of humans into male and female is the basis for the most elementary social classification everywhere."[2] "Social and political consequences are also acute in the society."[3] The Royal Commission on Labour, 1931, expressed its view. To be equal partners in national development women of India should be provided with the facilities of education, employment and health. The status of any community cannot be determined by not taking into account the health status of women and this can be understood according to social conditions which include basic needs like education, employment and health facilities which are unavailable or inaccessible due to poor infrastructure like transport and communication. Also rural PHCs are poorly equipped with basic facilities and medical staff. This can be achieved only by the strong will of the government, to implement the various legislature related to these overall basics.

Education is the base of all basics of the development process. So everything depends upon the application of education and simple training for improving women's health condition. The pace of women's education will have to be accelerated so that women also become aware of their rights. According to the 1991 census in the field of women's education there is some progress as compared to the 1981 census the 15.5 per cent women were more literate. Among women, Rajasthan has the lowest literacy rate, which comes to 20 per cent. In Rajasthan, the state of women education is further dismaying. The education in general percentage of men's education is two and half times more than literate women. Capabilities of women can be expanded by giving them education and make them literate. Education will enhance their ability to participate and contribute to the process of development. In the present chapter, socio-economic status and political background of elected women members have been discussed as it correlates with their political participation.

Education

The main hurdle in empowering the women is their illiteracy. The progress in women's education in India is far from satisfactory. In the modern period, our reformers and leaders and all our enlightened personalities had proclaimed the supreme importance of literacy and education. The need of the hour is not to repeat this rhetoric, but take practical steps to remove illiteracy. In recent years, we have made progress in the field through our various programmes. It is gratifying that the Ninth five-year Plan has given priority to the spread of elementary education.[4] Their confidence has to be developed in their own just and equitable worldview, to understand their present surroundings and thus empower them to change the oppressive position through their collective action. A scholar of nineteenth century, Mumtaj Ali, said, "An educated woman can take care of herself better than an inexperienced, uneducated, mentally confused bundle of veils which has not been allowed to develop self-confidence and cannot take care of herself." In fact the status of women in society is the indicator of a nation's overall development. m1p6

Swami Vivekananda said that there is no hope of rise for that family or country where there is no esteem for women, where they live in sadness. For this reason they have to be raised first. This can only be possible by educating them, because education improves the earning potential and productivity of women and helps them in asserting their rights.

Women's education is an essential element in a society. There has been a perceptible change in the political, economic and social status of women in the last 50 years, but we cannot claim that the progress is all that satisfactory. Education will play a major role in acquiring a certain "know How" in the social life of women. It will serve as a means by which women can interpret, analyse the environment around them and also help in making rational decisions. Government and political parties must be steadfast in their commitment to India's ancient culture, democracy and way of life, and the convenience and rights of women should be respected. Women should have the same opportunity as men to fulfil their ambitions.

Due to the treatment given by the society to the women there was widening gender gap and men with egoist thinking did not want women to come forward. Most women did not have the economic freedom to choose their life and career. Swami Vivekananda had observed, with his insight into our social reality, that the decline of India in the past was due to the monopolising of learning and education in the hands of a few sections of our society. While we cannot forget what happened in the past, what we are looking forward to is the future. Women are given priority as beneficiaries of government and programmes in rural areas. The majority of women have consequently experienced little benefit from development programmes.

Education will serve, as an indicator of confidence in women in giving strength and solidarity and an extraordinary and exciting development that will speed up their abilities to develop solutions for challenges coming in their way. It will help women in coordinating their activities with the others as much as possible, work for the people in the society and feel more connected to the rest of the population. It will facilitate women in formation of self-help groups for their economic empowerment and will help in mobilising them to challenge the gender-based social structure. It will also help in enabling them to recognise and exploit their potential, have access to government schemes and integrate the society.

The Constitution of India has brought the Indian women into a new era equipped with all rights and privileges and to enjoy the same rights which men do. Only proper and fruitful education can play the vital role and make women understand and aware about these rights which are specially formed for them.

While education is considered as an important opportunity for development of human capabilities, the deprivation of which in itself represent poverty, poverty of education or education poverty becomes an integral part of the human poverty. This is the dimension in which individuals shape their identities, and being able to give direction to their personal life is the central theme in empowerment. India's people are its best asset. The government should acknowledge this and work towards making it a reality and leave no stone unturned to solve the long-standing problems faced by them people. What is involved is the strength and the daring and the courage of the leaders. According to *World Report 1999-2000* about literacy of males of India,, is 67 per cent as compared to 82 per cent of world figure and for the females the adult literacy rate is 39 per cent as compared to 67 per cent for the females of the whole world. There is no change in male adult literacy rate in *World Report 2000-2001*. Gender disparity in adult literacy has declined. As rise in female adult literacy to one male adult literacy by 0.06 from 0.58 to 0.64 in one year can be seen as a positive factor in women empowerment. Education plays an important role in bringing women out of the boundaries of the household into the social and political world.

Graph 4.1

Educational Standard of Women Respondents

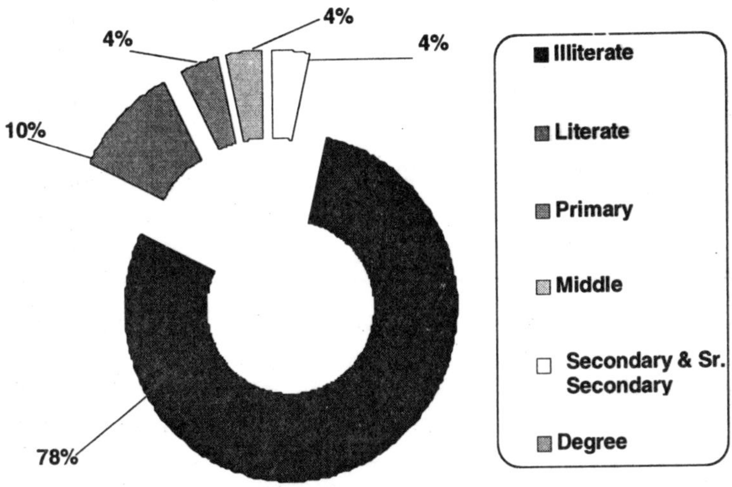

According to IHDR 1999 the all India literacy rate was 53 per cent with gender disparity of 0.62 whereas Rajasthan had total literacy at 58.5 per cent with 0.66 as gender disparity which is 0.04 better than the national level. It is further observed that gender disparity has a declining tendency when we take the lower age group, which is 0.92 in the age group 6-9, 0.86 in the age group 10-14 and 0.83 in the age group 15-19. It is heartening to observe that people are starting to think about giving education to the girl child. No section of society should feel that it is not being given social justice and protection. In fact, there is every reason to believe that women will be able to move forward. What is important for us is to keep the improvement intact. The improvement graph must go up. There is an urgent need to give the whole issue a rethink and decide on what the future should behold. There is need to stem the tide through a tremendous amount of awareness building and this should be our immediate objective.

Table 4.1
Status of Education

S.N.	*Qualification*	*Nos. of Women*	*Percentage*
1.	Illiterate	1	3.57
2.	Literate	22	78.57
3.	Primary (1-5)	3	10.71
4.	Middle (6-8)	–	–
5.	Secondary & Sr. Sec. (9-12)	1	3.57
6.	Degree	1	3.57
	Total	28	100

The above table and graph clearly depict the situation of education among elected women, as 23 out of 28 elected women whose percentage comes to 82 are illiterate and literate (who cannot read and understand but can only spell their names); 3 out of 28 have 11 as their overall percentage, 2(7 per cent) of the total women respondents have education secondary and above with one as a degree holder.

Table 4.2
Place of Education

S.N	*Designation*	*Rural*	*Urban*
1.	Pradhan	2 (7.14%)	1 (3.57%)
2.	Sarpanch	3 (10.71%)	–
3.	Ward panch	22 (78.57%)	–
	Total	27 (96.43%)	1 (3.57 %)

Age

Age is one of the determining factors in the emergence of leadership, particularly that of village leadership.[5] Age not only relates to the physical and mental make-up of an individual but also serves as an index of the individual's experience, awareness and wisdom in general. Traditionally age is considered an important factor in respect of one's status and prestige, particularly in rural societies. It was once the privilege of the older people to occupy the various key positions in the village.[6] Age is the vital factor to understand the demographic feature of the society. For the smooth functioning of society, there should be a balance of different age of groups of the society. An analysis of age groups will help one to understand the participatory attitude of the society in maintaining a balance between different age groups and will also give us a correct understanding of the proportion of the elected women in different age groups. For the purpose of study we have divided the age groups into five categories.

Graph 4.2

Distribution of Elected Women Members by Age

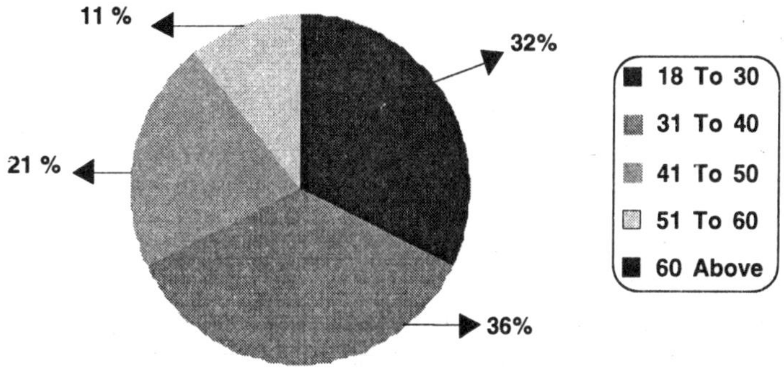

32.14 per cent, 35.71 per cent, 21.43 per cent, 10.71 per cent and zero percent represent the age group of 18 to 30, 31 to 40, 41 to 45, 46 to 50, 51 to 60 and 61 & above respectively. It is observed in the above table that Panchayati Raj has paved the way for the younger generation for participation in regional and national development.

Occupation

In the past employment of women was almost unthinkable. It was not liked by the society. If any woman dared take up a job, she was invariably a subject of social criticism and contempt and she was not considered a good woman. The people thought that an employed woman lacked virtue and dignity. Now a great change has taken place in the attitude of society towards employed women. Similarly, employment has taken place and there is a great increase in the confidence of women to take up jobs. Now the educated women feel that employment far from inviting dishonour, is a good source not only of income but also of social prestige and personal satisfaction.

Table 4.3

Distribution of Age

Age Group	*No. of Women*	*Percentage*
18 to 30	9	32.14
31 to 40	10	35.71
41 to 50	6	21.43
51 to 60	3	10.71
61 & above	–	–
Total	28	100

They feel that one income is generally not enough to satisfy the basic needs of the family. The economic condition of the family greatly improves if family members get employed and add to family income. An educated and employed woman feels that she has some prestige in the society and others listen to her with dignity. Moreover, she has sense of satisfaction that her education is not a waste and she is not useless for the family and the society.

It has been acknowledged that in poor communities, each member of the family has to contribute his or her mite to the economic activities. Among tribals, woman is an important contributor. The tribal women possess greater economic independence and freedom of movement than their counterpart in non-tribal societies cannot be disputed. Tribal women are as adept at agriculture, animal husbandry, forestry, etc., as their male counterpart. That tribal female is an overworked person and is conservative by nature. The overwhelming majority of rural women work in the agricultural sector cultivators marginal farmers and agricultural labours.

Graph 4.3

Occupation of Women Elected Members

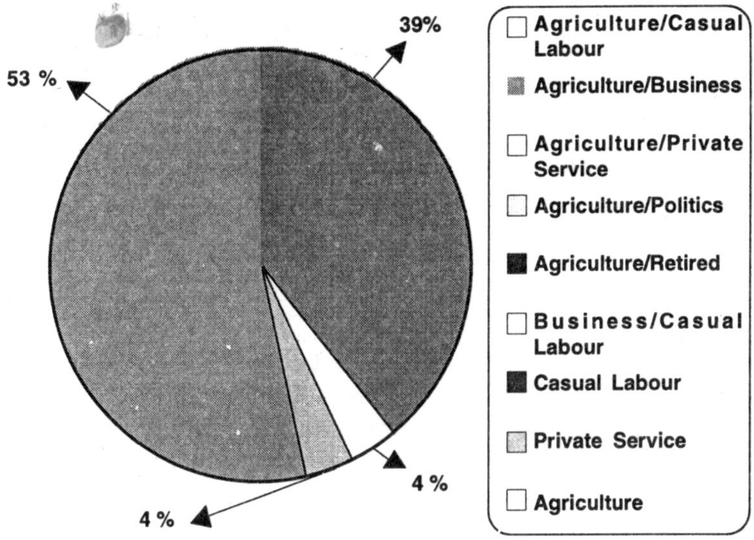

Employment is the deciding factor by way of which, quality of life of people can be measured, WPR'S as per IHDR 1999 based on the HDI survey 1994, all, India level, the male is 52.6 per cent, female is 26 per cent and the ratio of female-male comes to be 0.50, the work participation rate for Rajasthan male being 48 per cent, female 25.8 per cent and the ratio of female-male being 0.54. In Rajasthan women are doing better than an average Indian women worker but when we see it in the context of work participation the rate is the usual status which definitely affects more the income of any family. Rajasthan has female-male ratio of 0.22 as compared to 0.35 at the national level.

Table 4.4

Distribution of Occupation

S.No.	*Occupation*	*Nos. of Women*	*Percentage*
1.	Agriculture	15	53.57
2.	Agriculture /casual labour	11	39.29
3.	Agriculture / business	1	3.57
4.	Agriculture /private service	–	–
5.	Agriculture / politics	–	–
6.	Agriculture/ retired	–	–
7.	Business / casual labour	1	3.57
8.	Casual labour	–	–
9.	Private service	–	–
	Total	28	100

As the author found, out of 28 females 27 females are engaged in agriculture and other activities, 15 of them are engaged purely in agriculture and only two females are engaged in business with agriculture and working as casual labour.

Income

The income of the rural people on the average is lower than that of the urban people. This is because the volume of wealth of the rural community depends primarily on agriculture. The standard of life of the rural people on an average is lower than that of the urban people. Women of poorer section and those below the poverty line, are extremely overworked in both the field of earning out of the house and in housework. Being women and due to the nature of the job they do not go too far for their work. Women of lower class, working as an agriculture labourers, are getting low wages. The overpowering domination of males still persists. Wages of hard work done by women and wages for agriculture work when paid to women are taken over by men. In some regions where the husband-wife team or family labour is employed, the cash is handed over to the male. "Political freedom in India today is vibrant and unconfined, but the pursuit of social and economic freedom is still on, and the nation's efforts are focused on 'justice, social and economic' envisaged in the preamble, the fundamental rights and the directive principles of the constitution. We have to endeavour with sincerity and seriousness to remove every injustice, every discrimination from every quarter, and as the father of nation has put it, 'Wipe every tear from every eye'. (Speech of K.R. Narayanan on January 26, 1999). Biologically males and females have different physical structures but in rural economy females play a greater role besides looking after family affairs.

The income of the family of respondents is the important thing to know about their economic status. The income helps us to know about their living standards and the income of women respondent is one of the important factors. For our study we have tried to divide the income level into five categories. It shows the contribution of women in the economic status of the family.

Table 4.5

Income Position of the Elected Women Members

Level of Income	*Respondents*	*Percentage*
	Female	*Female*
Below Rs.1 000	5	17.86
Rs.1,001 to 3,000	19	67.86
Rs.3,001 to 5,000	2	7.14
Rs.5,001 to 8,000	2	7.14
Rs.8,000 to Above	–	–

The table gives us the picture of income of the family of the elected women respondents with 5 (17.86 per cent), 19 (67.86 per cent), 2 (7.14 per cent) and 2 (7.14 per cent), as below 1,000, 1,001 to 3,000, 3,001 to 5,000 and 5,001 to 8,000 per month respectively, which is very much satisfactory.

Land

According to census 2001 the rural population of India is 72.22 per cent and the rural population of Rajasthan is 76.62 per cent, which means that a majority of people depend upon agriculture as their main source of earning, and land is said to be main asset, which also plays a vital role in status in the society. Struggle over the question of land has, in fact, provided the main dynamic to the political life of the rural society in the present period. Different sections of the rural people hold different views on the land problems which are determined by their differing specific position in the socio-economic structure of the rural society. It is the principle source of employment and livelihood in the villages.

Land degradation affects the agricultural land and as a result agricultural productivity is declining sharply, while the number of family members to feed continues to grow in number. Heavy dependence on subsistence agriculture, lack of transport, communication and other development activities have kept the rural economy largely at the subsistence level. Changes in technology were largely responsible for many rural people leaving farms. The degradation of agricultural land significantly reduced the rural job market, resulting in migration. Rapidly increasing populations in the rural societies create unemployable surpluses of manpower that stream into the cities in search of work. High unemployment results in financial hardship and the cities also attract migrants because they offer a variety of jobs. There is increased migration of rural people to cities, peple leaving behind their land to be cultivated by other members of the family.

Agriculture has been the main occupation of the tribals, therefore land is their hope and glory. On the social side, the size of land holding of a person or family decides and determines the social status of the family to a certain extent.

The Above table show the extent of land holding—2(7.14 %), 5(17.86%), 12(42.86%), 5(17.86%) and 4(14.29%) are the number and percentage of land holdings of elected women members and their families. Land condition and irrigation facilities very much contribute to agriculture income; 4

(15.38%) own land without irrigation facility, 6 (23.08%) have partly irrigated land, 10 (38.46%) have wells for irrigating their land, the land of five of them (19.23%) is irrigated by canal water and 1(3.85%) has both canal and water facility, which seems to be satisfactory.

Table 4.6

Extent of Land Holding

No. of Bighas	*No. of Women*	*Percentage*
Landless	2	7.14
1 & 2	5	17.86
3 to 5	12	42.86
6 to 8	5	17.86
9 & Above	4	14.29
Irrigated: i) Well	10	38.46
ii) Nahar	5	19.23
iii) Both well & nahar	1	3.85
Not irrigated	4	15.38
Both irrigated & not irrigated	6	23.08

Family Structure

Tribal society is traditionally a nuclear family society. It is due to that in every family when a boy is married he is given a house built for him and is separated from the day he is married. This plays a great role in the economic condition and development because land and other belongings are also divided among the family members. A nuclear family is also the result of rural people migrating to urban areas.

Table 4.7

Type of Family

Type	*Respondents*	*Percentage*
	Female	*Female*
Nuclear	23	82.14
Joint	5	17.86

As we observe from the above table 23 (82.14%) of 28 women elected members live in nuclear family and only 5 (17.86%) live in joint family.

Marital Status

"Marriage lays the legal foundations for the family, but the family can exist without marriage. A family is a domestic group in which parents and children live together, and in its elementary form it consists of a couple with their children. This is often called the nuclear or elementary family."[7]

Table 4.8

Marital Status of the Women Elected Members

Particulars	*Respondents*	*Percentage*
	Female	*Female*
Married	26	92.86
Widow	2	7.14
Unmarried	–	–

Men enjoy more liberty, and they are free to do whatever they feel like; they do not need anyone's consent. A woman has no right to decision. Before marriage she is subservient to her father/brother and after marriage she is under the control of her husband and in-laws. A girl child's birth is not a welcome feature, because she is to be protected, and she cannot take up those jobs which a male can take and earn livelihood.[8] The degree of independence enjoyed by elected women representatives in decision making varies from case to case. In many cases male family members directed or at least guided the women. "Marriage is considered as the primary thing in the society because it is a must for the growth of generation."[9]

Party Affiliation

The political party affiliation may have an influence on the participation of an individual in political activities.

Membership of political party serves a dual purpose in developing the personality of an individual. On the one hand, through these institutions, he is able to relate himself to the political system, and at the same time develops a participant citizenship syndrome. On becoming a member of an institution, the person feels protected and close to the institutions of politics and government. He develops self-confidence that is a prerequisite of a modern citizen.

Graph 4.4

Party Affiliation of Elected Women Members

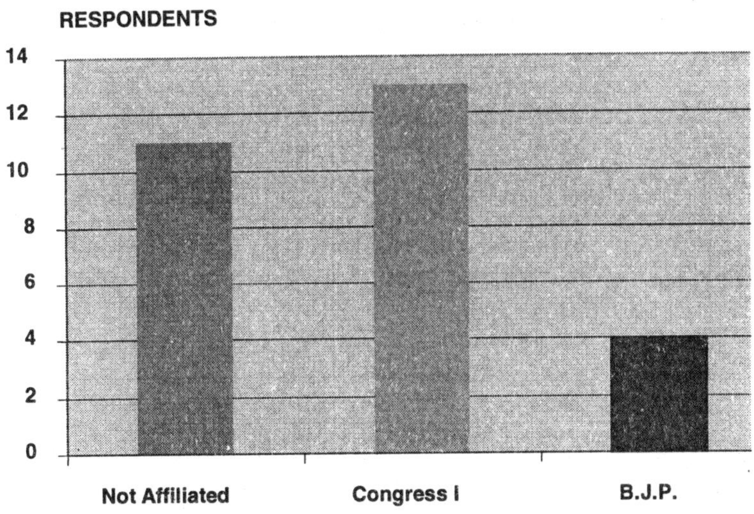

of these 60.71 per cent of total elected women members have acquired the political party's membership, out of which 46.43 per cent of the total women members are affiliated to the Congress, which has more influence in rural areas, and BJP has only 14.29 per cent of women members as its members; 39.29 per cent of the total women members have no affiliation with any political party, which means that more women nowadays are attracted by political parties, which is one of the factors of political participation.

Table 4.9
Party Affiliation

Particulars	*No. of Women*	*Percentage*
Not affiliated	11	39.29
Congress I	13	46.43
Bharatiya Janata Party	4	14.29
Total	28	100

WOMEN'S PARTICIPATION

When we study the working of Panchayati Raj institutions, it is the duty of us to study the women participatory role in these institutions in dealing with some aspects of development and empowerment. This means the study of working of these institutions and the actual role played by the women in solving the local problems, and also their influence on the decision making process in these institutions. Question regarding lack of women's capabilities of bearing responsibilities, reasons and suggestions to overcome these problems were asked. Some of the problems related to employment, accommodation and economic conditions. Besides these, they were suffering certain other handicaps like lack of education, illness and ignorance about their rights of those questioned, 48.48 per cent and 18.18 per cent of male and female respectively said lack of education; 10.60 per cent and 7.57 per cent of male and female respectively cited health; 24.24 per cent and 12.12 per cent of male and female respectively said lack of self-confidence and self-decision were main hurdles in women's participation. Women's confidence has to be developed in their own just and equitable worldview, to understand their present surroundings and thus empower them to change the oppressive position through their collective action. Giving them training can expand capabilities of elected women representatives. Workshops for elected women representatives will provide them opportunities to understand the issues before the village panchayats, their role in the social and political empowerment of women to intervene in their matters, and also the role of panchayats in improving their lot.

Table 4.10

Role of Women Members towards Responsibility

	Respondents		Percentage	
	Male	*Female*	*Male*	*Female*
Able to bear their responsibility	25	28	37.87	42.42
Unable to bear their responsibility	13	–	19.69	–

Table 4.10

Reasons for Inability to bear Their Responsibility

	Respondents		Percentage	
	Male	*Female*	*Male*	*Female*
1. Lack of education	7	–	10.60	–
2. Dependency	4	–	6.06	–
3. Lack of self-decision	2	–	3.03	–

To strengthen the economic position of Panchayats, to enable them to play a meaningful role in social transformation in the rural areas, a state-level two-day workshop on 21-22 May 2004, for elected women representatives of Panchayati Raj institutions belonging to Scheduled Castes was organised by the Rajasthan government at the Indira Gandhi Panchayati Raj Evam Grameen Vikas Sansthan, Jaipur, under the National Women's Commission.

Speaking at the valedictory function, the Panchayat Secretary, Panchayati Raj and Rural Development Department, M.K. Khanna said, "The Panchayats should be made self-reliant, especially on the economic front, so that they could play an influential role at the local level." He also underlined the significance of imparting regular training to the elected representatives on the identified themes.

Table 4.12

Respondents' Suggestions to Women Members

Variables of Suggestion	*Respondents*		*Percentage*	
	Male	*Female*	*Male*	*Female*
Education	32	12	48.48	18.18
Health	7	5	10.60	7.57
Group discussion	4	1	6.06	1.51
Employment	3	–	4.54	–
Self confidence & self-decision	16	8	24.24	12.12
Having no suggestions	3	4	4.54	6.06

G.S. Somawat, Director of the National Commission for Scheduled Castes in Rajasthan, said, "The lack of literacy among the elected women representatives of Panchayats was a major stumbling block to their effective functioning." He called for holding regular training programmes for women representatives in the state to overcome this adequacy."[10]

Since ancient times women's rightful place as citizens in the mainstream of the society has been ignored. They were considered incapable of knowing what was best for them. Since primitive ages women were treated as weaker sex of the human race. It is so not only in India but in Western countries. In Western countries women were empowered long ago but in India the concept and process of empowering of women has started lately . For the upliftment of women, efforts are being given through education and legislation, which have put women on par with men. The strategic objective of women's education and human rights education may be explained as probing into the cause of deterioration in the development of women empowerment and introduction of measures aimed at improving trust, cooperation and understanding between other sections of society (male), and also strengthening the existing human rights mechanism and develop practical action oriented measures and strategies to fight intolerance. Empowerment of women in robust sense of priorities should be taken as a thought, a principle, a way of life, a movement. Everyone including women should vow to finish this as a mission to secure and rebuild the country and everyone should know this mission. There is some attention being paid by political parties and governments to the plight of women since last few years which is awelcome development. State and central governments have focused on reservation for women in educational institutions and jobs, introduced special schemes like the development of women and children in rural areas, extended credit for self-employment schemes for groups of women, boosted their socio-economic development by setting up self-help groups and their participation in development schemes. Therefore, there is a need for efforts to accelerate the process of bringing equality and development of women. Women's participation in Panchayati Raj can play an important role in becoming an effective tool of empowerment of women. Reservation of seats for women in PR Institutions has encouraged them for active involvement in the political process of the country. It has provided an opportunity for them to participate in decision making and implementation processes in rural society.

The image of an institution more or less depends upon its performance. Therefore, the perception of elected women members were taken to rate the performance of Panchayati Raj. In India women's studies is more closely affected by central and state governments' policies and programmes, and the role of education in women studies is its most important aspect because it has an impact on change. It is also likely that numerous factors like the agricultural economy, employment, social welfare and women's issues, and most importantly education, will make an equal impact in empowering women. Greater coordination of health, employment, welfare and education interventions will have an effect on the status of women and girls, and for this education is considered to be an asset for raising the status, dignity and self-confidence of women and girls. It must, however, be noted that most women in rural as well as in the urban areas are not fully participating in the economic, political and social fields since they are not being educated due to the old social values continuing to be inhibiting.

Detailed probing into the causes of sharp deterioration in development of women empowerment and introduction of measures aimed at improving trust, cooperation and understanding between communities (gender-wise) have successfully helped us to embrace the rich cultural diversity of the great nation of ours. Women's participation in the political process is central to their struggle against oppression, and participation of women is certainly a positive force. Empowering women through reservation has changed the orientation, and more women in politics would definitely be an asset. The question of representation for women had over the years, since independence, been a debatable subject. The 73rd and 74th amendments in the Constitution provide one-third reservation for women nationwide in Panchayati Raj.

Recognising the importance of democratic institutions at the grassroots level, Article 40 in Part-IV (Directive Principles of State Policy) of the Constitution has stated that the state shall take steps to organise village Panchayats and endow them with such powers and authority as may be necessary to enable them to function as units of self-government. The states have established Gram Panchayats for villages or groups of villages with civic and economic activities for a village community as one of the functions. Women's participation in grassroots democracy has widely been recognised. Participation of women is an integral part of democratic process and strengthening the quality of civic life. As they are half the population, women must participate in decision making in all socio-economic and political organisations. The Balwant Rai Mehta Committee Report (1957) recommended induction of two women members in every Panchayat to carry out the specific programmes of development of women and children.

'Some of the elected women representatives attended training sessions. NGOs in particular focused on training for women representatives. Most women had no previous experience with such training sessions and could not significantly improve their knowledge and awareness on legal literacy issues through the training, but might have gained self-esteem and experience by getting the freedom to attend such training. The women generally appreciated the training session because the attendance involved a social gathering with other women of the area.'[11]

To provide enhanced representation to the rural women in Panchayati Raj institutions, certain specific provisions have been incorporated in the Constitution through the seventy-third Amendment Act. This Amendment to the Constitution of India has created a legitimate political space for women to establish governance at the grassroots for the purpose of achieving social justice and economic development. Occupying the space by the rustic womenfolk is not an easy task though it is legitimate for them. It provides that not less that one-third of the total members of offices of chairpersons in the Panchayats at each level shall be reserved for women. The participation of women in the PRIs has increased. This increase in participation of women may be due to the Seventy-Third Amendment Act, but it has brought a new wave of enthusiasm, amongst them. The 73rd Amendment through Panchayati Raj institutions is focused and emphasizes on women's share of power in politics. The act provides reservation for women with a minimum of one-third of total seats to be filled by direct election including seats reserved for Schedule Caste and Scheduled Tribes and also with a minimum of one-third seats reserved for Sarpanchs, Pradhans and Zila Pramukhs, which means that women's representation should be always more that 33 per cent in the Panchayati Raj institution.

In terms of number approximately eight lakh women shall be elected members of Panchayat as Panchs. There would be approximately 7,5000, 1,500 and 150 women as Sarpanchs, Pradhans and Zila Pramukhsa respectively. This gender justice provided to women will have a tremendous impact and will change the nature of politics. This reservation should not be limited as just an opportunity given to the women but it should work as women's leadership build-up. Thus it is more significant in case of women whose level of political consciousness is on an increase. Educated women had significant effect on their attitude. Women who are educated bring up their children better. With the increasing political consciousness women are becoming more aware about the development process and its impact on their socio-economic status and taking part therein. These members only define the 73rd Amendment. But it is very important to study the impact of this act. Whether women's participation increased can only be assessed by their education, health and other facilities.

Induction as Panchayat Member

Women were seen in the ancient scriptures as equal partners of men in all aspects of life, material and spiritual. Women consisting half of the human population have been treated as the weaker sex in all societies of the world. It is evidently true that our society is a male-dominated society and women were treated as a household commodity who looked after the family affairs and in recent times too to some extent are treated likewise. Women still face many obstacles in their right for representation, and the number of elected women continues to be used as rubber stamps. Women should enter political parties in large numbers and work towards bringing about internal democracy and transparency of functioning. Women and men have to join hands to secure universal human rights. Unless women are empowered in India any significant decrease in birth rate, death rates, infant mortality rates and the malnutrition rates cannot be anticipated. Women in India are treated as vulnerable section of the society. "The tradition of Indian rural society is that man is superior to woman. Keeping in line with this tradition, the leadership in villages seemed to be male dominated."[12] No doubt, changes are taking place from one corner of the country to another corner but the intensity is different in every state. The development process has ignored her. The economic and social standing of tribal women has been deteriorating. Action consists of the structures and processes by which human beings form meaningful intention and, more or less successfully, implement them in a concrete system. The outcome of every good work is a lesson for society. In this kind of system every person is the subject and object of the action. It can be said that every decision taken affects the whole social structure. In every country's democratic parliament leaders used to take every decision affecting the development of the society or the people.

The social system is made up of the interaction among every individual. Society is the special kind of social system and in every society there are differences in power between every human beings. Power is given by the society and this makes a difference in the gender. Gender differentiation in India is perhaps the most severe problem that the country is facing today. There is a need to uplift women's position and status in society. There is a silver lining in every dark cloud and in India, women is being benefited in various spheres of life by way of many schemes. She is helped in trying to come out from her age-old inferiority complex, and for this, education is rightly considered the panacea for all ills. "Every woman is a fountain of Shakti or Power and Energy but the boulders that have blocked its exuberance have to be removed to allow this stream to flow freely once again. Women will then march on their own to realisation and manifestation," are the words of Swami Vivekananda. Mahatma Gandhi, who was a man of foresight, saw in women the great qualities of patience, endurance, the capacity to sacrifice and sufferings. He understood the dormant potentialities of women and made all efforts to awaken them to rise to the occasion. Some of the very basic measures of far-reaching significance that we have taken of late are the constitutional amendments establishing Panchayati Raj and local self-government and giving one-third representation to women in these grassroots democratic bodies. These have made a creative stir in our society and is an important step in the participation of the ordinary people in local government and development, and in the empowerment of women. It was disheartening to note that the position of women has not improved much yet. "If the husband has a high-status job compared to his wife (who may have no job outside the home), a better education than his wife, or more organisational and management skills, then he will have more power in decision making in the family."[13]

India is a gender segregated society, and to change this image it will take some time. Women are still dominated by the males, especially at the grassroots level. This is due to the fact that most of the female members are illiterate and most of them have contested the election for the first time. In many cases, they have done so because the seats were reserved for them and their husbands/sons wanted them to contest election since they themselves could not contest for the seats reserved for women. The participation of women in the PRIs has increased. Though the increase in participation of women may be due to the Seventy-third Amendment Act, yet it has brought a new wave of enthusiasm amongst them. We also found that the women members have become active and they take keen interests in the works of the DPC.

Equality and equity of women cannot be alienated from development. As already indicated, women performed some of the most important and strenuous outdoor jobs. There can be no sustainable development without giving equal status to the half of the population that is women. Equality of women means that women should be given the opportunity as men regarding health care, education, work participation and above all the decision making with seats in parliament, state assemblies and local level government. Ashok Celly has rightly asserted, "Women's participation in politics is necessary for holistic development. Women are bound to have a better perspective on vital issues such as environment, health care and education, particularly of the girl child, as these affect them directly."

"Twenty-five per cent of women had remarked on visible change in their status within their family after having been elected, about 60 per cent of women said that they would encourage women to stand for election, the same percentage is contemplating to contest PRI election again", revealed a report of the Society for Participatory Research in Asia, February, 2000. The change in the attitude of women has brought a positive role in their social identities and political awareness among them.

If membership in Panchayats which are only implementing agencies of the decisions and policies decided in state capitals and at centre have brought so much confidence in the women then if women are given their full dues and reservation in parliament and state assemblies where all policies are formed that will be helpful in creating an urge among them to become part and parcel of political, economic and social life.

Since independence it can be seen that 47 (8.8 per cent) women were elected in parliament in 1994 out of 543 seats which is the highest, in 1997 with 19 (3.5 per cent) women out of 542 seats was the lowest.

To bring women into the political mainstream the Women's Reservation Bill was presented in parliament many times but could not be passed because of the will of politicians who think this as an encroachment on male dominance. Over the five decades since independence, a consensus has not been reached among the political parties regarding providing reservation to women in parliament and state assemblies. Some political parties raise the issues of reservation to women in parliament, only eyeing the vote bank, but when it comes to legislation they keep themselves away and oppose on some flimsy ground.

Government has launched many programmes for upliftment of women as a policy matter and empowering them through reservation to deal with the problem. Central and state governments are putting in efforts to uplift women's position, but even then the position of rural women the continues to be low. The successive governments have shown a lack of political will to implement the laws which previous governments had formulated. There is no awareness shown by the government and there is poor performance by important institutions of the government. This current environment has so adversely affected growth. But these measures can be effective only when women get real benefit from these. It is found that most of womanfolk are either unaware of these steps taken by government or are unable to take advantage of these schemes. The future of women would be very bright only if they adopt high education as a weapon.

Women who are elected in legislative assembly or parliament through their influential background become a part of this hierarchy. They have no motivation or incentive to challenge the hierarchy of political parties or bring about any change.

No longer are women content to remain passive spectators of the development process of the country. Women's efforts to gain greater political power have made at least some progress. The women representatives of Panchayati Raj are very happy that now they are being involved in the planning process. But it is disheartening to note that only a few members have the knowledge about the Reservation Policy. A radical change can take place only when the women of India realise that they themselves possess the power to alter their situation. Education will not only give women the much-needed confidence and equip them to face the challenges of a changing work environment it is a process of acquiring knowledge to live with dignity in a society. This will lead them towards awareness of rights, effective political participation and a better quality of life. Even though women have to go a long way, a beginning has been made.

Ninth Five Year Plan (1997-2002) Commitment towards Women

— To create an enabling environment for women to exercise their rights, both with and outside home, as equal partners along with men, through early adoption of 'National Policy for Empowerment of Women'.

— To legislate reservation of not less than one-third seats for women in the Lok Sabha and in the State Legislative Assemblies and thus ensure adequate representation of women in decision making.

— To adopt an integral approach towards empowering women through effective convergence of existing service, resources, infrastructure and manpower in both women-specific and women-related sectors.

— To adopt a special strategy of 'Women's Component Plan' to ensure that not less than 30 per cent of funds/ benefits flow to women from other developmental sectors.

— To organise women into self-help groups and thus mark the beginning of a major process of empowering women.

— To accord high priority to reproductive child health services and thus ensure access to maternal and child health service.

— To universalise the ongoing supplementary feeding programme-special Nutrition Programme (SNP) and Mid-Day Meals (MDM).

— To ensure easy and equal access to education for women and girls through the commitments of the Special Action Plan of 1998.

— To initiate steps to eliminate gender bias in all educational programmes.

— To institute plans for free education for girls up to the college level, including professional courses.

— To equip women with necessary skills in the modern upcoming trades which could keep them gainfully engaged besides making them economically independent and self-reliant

— To increase access to credit through setting up of a 'Development Bank for Women Empowerment' in small and tiny sectors.

Concluding Observations

The concluding observations made during the field survey by are as follows:

1) Report regarding voting in parliamentary and assembly election—68.18 and 72.73 per cent respectively.
2) Report always voting in local election—86.36 per cent.
3) Active in at least one organisation involved in community problems—54.55 per cent.

4) Have worked with others in trying to solve some community problems—59.09 per cent.
5) Have attempted to persuade others to vote as they were—81.82 per cent.
6) Have ever actively worked for a party or candidates during an election—72.73 per cent.
7) Have ever contracted a local government official about some issue or problem—36.36 per cent.
8) Have attended at least one political meeting or rally in the last three years—90.91 per cent.
9) Have ever contracted a state or national government official about some issue or problem —54.55 per cent.
10) Have ever formed a group or organisation to attempt to solve some local community problem—40.91 per cent.
11) Have ever given money to a party or candidate during an election campaign—31.82 per cent.
12) Presently a member of a political club or organisation—40.91 per cent.

References

1. Arti Mishra, *Women in Slums: Impact of Environmental Pollution*, Classing Publishing Company, New Delhi, 2004, p.68.
2. Lucy Mair, *An Introduction to Social Anthropology*, Oxford University Press, London, 1972, p.54.
3. Bishwanath Ghosh, The Menace of Educated Unemployment in Search of a Strategy, *Industrial Times*, January 12, 1973, p.17.
4. *The Times of India*. JAN 26, 1999 speech of K. R. Narayanan on the eve of 26 January, 1999.
5. H.C. Srivastav, *Dysfunctional Para-Politics and Elite Action in India,* Bharatiya Vidya Prakashan, Varanasi, 1967, p.27.
6. S.R. Mehta, *Emerging Pattern of Rural Leadership*, Wiley Eastern Private Limited, New Delhi, 1972, p.80.
7. Lucy Mair, op. cit., 1972, p.94.
8. *Social Action*, A Quarterly Review of Social Trends, October-December, Vol. 51, No. 4, 2001, p.366.

9. Arti Mishra, op. cit.
10. *The Hindu*, Sunday, May 23, 2004, p.5.
11. Berthold Kuhn, *Participatory Development in Rural India*, Radiant Publishers, New Delhi, 1998, p.254.
12. G.D. Bhatt, *Emerging Leadership Pattern in Rural India—An Empirical Study*, New Delhi, M. D. Publication Pvt. Ltd., 1994, p.131.
13. Walter A. Friedlander, Robert Z. Apte, *Introduction to Social Welfare*, Prentice Hall Inc., U.S.A., 1982.

5

Education and Society

Education is indisputably the most effective way to shape values, attitudes, behaviours and skills that will equip the people to act in the long-term interests of the country. It is a thought, a principle, a way of life, a movement. It will greatly enhance one's ability to acquire and retain knowledge.

Education plays an important role in the acquisition of political status and is also important as the prime indicator of changes in every area of life. Education is the basic postulate in the development of any society, nation and civilisation. Without education a man remains a rustic. It creates the courage and ability to deal with adverse situations successfully and more opportunities to expand oneself and one's personality. "I am the master of my fate, I am the captain of my soul", are well versed by poet Hanely. A person's attitude shapes his future, his thoughts determine his destiny. He can translate his thoughts into reality only through education. You just have to be yourself. "Education has always been important, because education and literacy help man to build a sound personality, make a person more rational, liberating him from representatives and make him socially conscious and vigilant."[1]

Though literacy is not exactly synonymous with education, it can be taken as indicator of tribal awareness to education. Literacy is only a crude indicator of education. Since education is probably the most effective instrument for ensuring equality of opportunity, the tribals lag far behind their counterparts in the country due to lack of education.

"However nobody would probably deny that 'education' of the right type would help and 'education' is important in order that social change is made possible".[2] It is, therefore, necessary to examine the level of education attained by the tribals. Since education is probably the most effective instrument for ensuring equality of opportunity, the tribal people are lagging far behind their more fortunate fellow countrymen due to lack of education. Education of the tribal people of India can hardly be isolated from the problem of general education. Education can play a very important role in the socio-economic development of tribals. Our aim should be to clear the cobwebs in people's mind and bring about a change in the mindset and the common perception and once we set out to achieve all this, we can truly say that we are shaping the attitude of our youth positively and giving them a push in the right direction as education largely employs the interdisciplinary approach.

"The term 'education' has been interpreted differently by different philosophers. But the importance of education has always been realised by all people at all times."[3] If the education is to be dynamic, it must reflect the social growth and works as catalyst in taking some initiative and responsibility for social progress. Education is a creative force; it must be forged ahead and it will supply new ideas that will reconstruct and revitalise the social fabric that prevails. According to Durkheim, the major function of education is the transmission of society's norms and values. "Society can survive," he says, only if there exists among its members a sufficient degree of homogeneity, education perpetuates and reinforce this homogeneity by fixing in the child from the beginning essential similarities which collective life demands."[4]

Educational Standards

It is important to provide the benefits of development and to put constitutional responsibilities above everything. This has to be done to make it more representative which will serve as an indicator of confidence in the strength and solidarity and bring in more development. Education is the platform for human development. We need to modify our education system to promote lateral thinking and innovation. The objective of education is the all-round development of the human personality—physical, intellectual, mental and emotional. To achieve the ideal such an all-round development is essential.[5]

Table 5.1

Educational Standards

	Respondents		*Percentage*	
	Male	*Female*	*Male*	*Female*
Illiterate	–	1	–	1.51
Literate	6	22	9.09	33.33
Primary (1-5)	11	3	16.16	4.54
Middle (6-8)	4	–	6.06	–
Secondary & Sr. Secondary (9-12)	16	1	24.24	1.51
Degree	1	1	1.51	1.51

Education is a platform for students where they could get involved with issues through culture. It would change mindsets and soon become quality education in the entire world. It is further suggested that a people's committee should be set up in every Panchayat to conduct resource mapping under the auspices of the elected Panchayat committees. Volunteers should be selected and given training in survey research and preparation of sector-wise status report. This will help the Panchayats to identify and realise the real demands of the Panchayats and availability of resources. The educational environment of the family plays an important role in motivating the younger generation to obtain education. Individuals who have been able to attain a certain level of education usually aspire for their children at least as much as or higher than their own level of educational achievement. Many a time, the parents' education is used as an indicator of the educational environment of the family.

Formal Education and Its Values

Education refers to the method by which a society attempts to direct and accelerate the learning process of its members. Formal education is a way to the notion of lifelong learning. "Formal education refers to schooling— an organised system of training for developing knowledge, skills, mind, character etc. of individuals. Informal education emanates from an individual's own experience and continues through out his life. However with the development and use of organised source of mass media for 'education', the distinction between formal and informal education hinges on enrolment specified structural instructional programme spread over a period of time, examination and certification. In this monograph, the term 'education' is used in its narrower sense; it refers to literacy and formal schooling."[6]

Formal education is very much necessary for the members of tribal societies to discharge their social obligations. This is a well known fact that education in India has spread in a haphazard way without taking care of future needs. No study can be complete unless the government policy with respect to education is highlighted. "Education does not proceed in a vacuum; its character is determined by the group culture and schools, institutions created by society to attain certain specific ends."[7] Indian education has suffered considerably because of two things. One, the lack of means of transportation and communication. Two, the lack of educational values. Schools were scattered at far off distances. Each school was meant to serve a good area. Due to of the lack of good roads and other means of transportation, even some of those who really wish for education benefit from it.

The goal and objectives of education at different stages and spheres should be reoriented or structured so that education and society would move closer to each other. "While there are absolute objectives of education which are universal consisting of the harmonious development of the personality of the child, the building up of his character and helping him to prepare himself to face the tasks of life, each country at each time has also to identify the national goal and organise the education process to achieve them."[8]

Programmes of educational reconstruction would constitute a major plank of educational policy. "Large number of the tribals are still unaware of the facilities and programmes for specialised and higher education. In spite of lack of knowledge regarding facilities for education and special programmes of assistance to the tribals, it seems that a fairly large proportion of the tribals perceive importance of educating their children."[9]

"More allocation of funds and opening of schools do not go far in providing education to the people. Social factors play a very important role in this respect. Formal education has not been necessary for the members of tribal societies to discharge their social obligations. Hence they should be prepared to accept education and it should be presented to them in such a way as to cut the barriers, superstition and prejudices."[10] Formal education in its meaning involves instruction in specially designated school premises where knowledge could be retained and given by more people to more and more people. "The idea of education—impiying the structural transmission of knowledge within a formal institution—is giving way to a broader notion of 'learning' that takes place in diversity of settings."[11] There is great scope to consolidate growth momentum with special emphasis on education and employment generation. There is an urgent need to give the whole issue a rethink and decide on what the future should behold. All efforts would be made to improve the functioning of the sector, which is so vital for the economy. We should identify areas where improvements could be made and initiate necessary steps to further streamline and strengthen the sector. An integrated, time-bound action plan should soon be drafted to promote infrastructure for education.

Education and Leadership

The primary work of leadership is to release body, mind, heart and spirit towards great purposes. They communicate to people their worth and potential so clearly that they are inspired to see it in themselves. They facilitate the way for helping people to optimise their capacities and potential.

They allow others to fulfil their purpose and contribution for the benefit of both individual and organisation.

Table 5.2

Respondent's Opinion regarding Education

Opinion	*Respondents*		*Percentage*	
	Male	*Female*	*Male*	*Female*
No. of schools should be less	2	2	3.03	3.03
More (upgrade or anganwari)	4	5	6.06	7.57
New schools should be open	12	3	18.18	4.54
Nos. are quite right	21	13	31.81	19.69
No comment	–	3	–	4.54
Others	10	2	15.15	3.03

These principles are the foundation for creating lives. It is only through education that one's personality undergoes an all-round development and develops a purposive and all-round outlook on the world around one. It is essential for the leader to have some standard of literacy. We can all see ourselves as catalyst both at home and at work. It is necessary to combine theory with practical training. Introspection, self-examination and self-perception are essential for all, but more so for those who are leading society and who are occupying seats for power and authority.[12] The knowledge, skills and commitment determine the organisation's success. Leaders who optimise their work are the key to sustained success.

People who are chosen usually don't have the skills, the orientation or the aspiration to understand when things go wrong. The key factor is that they have the responsibility but not the knowledge and authority. They can suffer from lack of being able to communicate. The most basic of the job is taking care of all the day-to-day problems. Most of the uneducated leaders do not have the fundamental knowledge of public dealing, they have poor decision-making abilities and they fail to initiate any development programme or redress the grievances of the people. Educational development is a participatory process and it will help them to understand the rules, regulations and fulfil the objectives of Panchayati Raj institutions. They can help them in carrying out their day-to-day functions and also help in the development of personality, social mobility and change in occupation. Every person has in him the potential to excel and create a favourable environment. Both these reasons make it obligatory for them to have education. In view of the poor standard of literacy and poor knowledge of various matters, it is desirable that members should be instructed thoroughly about their duties and functions. Although there are training centres for members, a few days, training is not sufficient for them. Sometimes refreshers courses are also held but that are rarely organised since government is always running short of fund, and these trainings serve a temporary purpose. Besides training, members must be served with written instructions clearly pointing out their duties and rights, powers and functions.

Our experience has shown that a multidimensional approach towards family and community betterment with emphasis on education, skill development, income generation and women's development works more effectively than laws as rightly said by Earl Warren. One lone individual's character can make a difference in his or her circle of influence. This comes from a sense of belonging to his surroundings, an involvement with his people. Politically aware everyone has an opinion and sometimes can be too opinionated and even the grassroots get involved. Education increases the degree of political participation, which is the essence of political development. Our aim is granting the people a significant role and to work for possible political responsibility. If leaders study the entire scenario dispassionately they will visualise the substantial synergy. The political situation in the country has inevitably its effect on its educational system.

Education, Mass Media and Communication

Indian education has suffered considerably by lack of transportation and communication as schools are scattered at far off distances. One of the communication vehicles is education, through which suggestions are submitted and studied seriously and acted on, and where feedback is fast and effective. Each school is meant to serve a good area but lack of good roads and other means of transportation for some of those who really wish for education cannot reap the benefits of it. In the tribal and agricultural society man is bound by the world of the tribe or the village. He hardly needs to know about the world outside. But today tribal men as well as village men have to look upon themselves as members of the Indian nation. This big transformation in outlook may be traced to the processes, which started in the beginning of the nineteenth century. The introduction of modern education, the improvement in the means of transportation and communication, and the establishment of a central political authority, have all been helping in the process of nation building.[13]

Areas with the scantiness of roads and means of communication were the real hurdles in the way of the expansion of education. Much of the social change revolves round roads and transport. Due to this fact, the Auxiliary Committee Review carried the optimistic remarks: "Concurrent with the numerical expansion, there has been a slow, but steady breakdown of the obstacles that stood in the way of the spread of education. The isolation of rural areas and the difficulties imposed by distance on the extension of education are gradually being lessened by the building of new roads and railways, and by the provision of motor services, which are linking up even remote villages with the main stream of life and activity." According to Lerner: "... no modern society functions efficiently without a developed system of mass-media."[14] Lerner also found in his study of the Middle East that, "Literacy and media participation are highly correlated."[15] Mass communication has become today a means of various types of knowledge. Education plays a major role in the utilisation of mass media. "Since each person responds according to acquired knowledge, education is a pre-condition for the effective use of the mass-media. Conversely, the lack of education is a constraint on the utilisation of the mass-media."[16] Education and mass media help in accelerating the pace of change. The mass media is the device that can spread the requisite knowledge and attitude quickly and widely, and without it we can miss the uptodate knowledge of the modern world.

According to Lerner, modernisation and economic development involve three phases—growth in urbanisation, growth in literacy and finally, growth in mass media. All these three are linked together in the modern society. "National development depends upon a change in knowledge—what people know; skills — what people can do; and attitude — what people can aspire for and hope to get. This is the reason why in the recent decades education, including mass communication, is looked upon as an investment. This basic change in knowledge, skills and attitudes among the citizens of the country help in increasing its productivity."[17] The man with a mobile personality becomes free from his bonds to the native soil and desires to move from the field to the factory and from the farm house to the urban flat.[18]

"While one need not be literate in order that he is able to receive and understand a communication, literacy probably defines a threshold for social action in the sense that those who are literate are probably more amenable to social change than those who are not. It is granted that illiterate and uneducated people can be organised for radical social actions—but the participants here, sometimes may not understand clearly the goals and process of social action."[19] There are growing opportunities for individuals, throughout their lifetimes, to engage in learning activities and training outside traditional classroom. The educated people develop a capacity to identify themselves with new aspects of their environment when exposed to mass media. Educating the people is a constructive attempt to find solutions, and empower ordinary citizens to use the right to information as a powerful weapon, and it will lay the foundation for better decision making and communication.

Education and Political Parties

In recent decades, various political parties have sprung up in the rural area. These parties struggle among themselves to win the support of the rural people with a view to gaining control over the state. Political parties are a medium of struggle for power, and at the same time it is an agency to give political education to the people. In a democratic country political parties obviously play a vital role. The level of political consciousness promoted by the political education programme of the party inspires political action, which throws up new political leaders. The process of building up leadership, the channelisation of struggle for power and the political education for masses all go hand in hand with the political parties. The bigger and national political parties play an important role in the assignment of political positions, which sometimes go against the interests of the tribals. It is, therefore, also necessary for the rural people to study the programmes and policies of these political parties. For these reasons, it makes it obligatory for them to have education.

Education and Human Rights

It is known fact that the value of education operates in a cumulative manner. Illiteracy often comes in the way of ensuring human rights of all individuals, so we have to make efforts and a beginning in this desired direction. Particularly in our country around half of the growth is due to rural-urban migration, which itself is mainly the result of stagnant development in the countryside and the lack of prospects for the younger generation.

Every person would be able to get his piece of cake only through political awareness and an active participation in the public life, which is possible by education. Education would promote knowledge, values, attitudes and skills conducive to respect for human rights, to an active commitment to the defence of such rights and to the building of a culture of peace and democracy. Education provides not only jobs, but also gives them the aptitude to be conscious of their rights. Law cannot be self-applied and can help ensure equality and justice only in a favourable atmosphere by awareness followed by educating each village and individual.

The legislation could help ensure equality and justice only in a favourable atmosphere through awareness followed by education. Education has some connection with awareness of law. There is need to stem the tide through a tremendous amount of awareness building. The rural man needs to know a minimum of law, governing judicial and administrative process as well as powers of various state organs. An educated person is more conscious of his rights as well as his duties, as a citizen of his country.

Education and Gender Disparity

Today every person should be viewed as a partner in the common task of nation building. Education as an advocate of values and principles in politics will take meaningful steps to establish coordination between procedures and time-frame implementation of measures, which would take care of all the woes. The adverse sex ratio is 922 (910) women to 1,000 men in the state. There are also wide regional variations, with the sex ratio ranging from 821(807) women per 1,000 in Jaisalmer, 828 (795) in Dholpur, 857 (832) in Bharatpur, 889 (854) in Sawai Madhopur, 877 in Sri Ganganagar, 887 (880) in Alwar and 895 (881) in Kota. It is very evident that education has changed the attitude of people towards women. While it is difficult to calculate the contribution of education in the field of economics it contributes most in fostering a new attitude in the people. The educational development of the female is much lower than that of the males. According to Census 2001 only two districts out of 32—Jhunjhunun and Kota—have the highest female literacy, which comes in the range of 60 to 70 per cent, five districts including five the state capital Jaipur fall in the range of 50 to 60 in female literacy; 12 districts are in the range; 40 to 50; 11 and 1 districts fall in ranges 30 to 40 and 20 to 30 respectively.

Our policies have to be intrinsically linked to various events and hence, we will be fully aware of what is happening and this would enable us to appropriately prepare ourselves for the future. The government should take steps towards capacity-building programmes, to face the emerging challenges, by devoting itself in promoting human development in key areas such as literacy, woman and child development, and health for the benefit of the common man. It should focus on promotion of grassroots democracy through Panchayati Raj giving particular attention to providing opportunities to the underprivileged and the deprived. There should be a serious move towards exploring as to what will be the best possible way of doing it.

The Elementary Education Programme initiatives focused in providing education to tribals, school dropouts and girl children. According to the Education Commission (1964-66) "for full development of our human resources, the importance of homes and for moulding the character of children during most impressionable years of infancy, the education of women is of even greater importance than that of men. In the modern world the role of women goes much beyond the home and she is now adopting a career of her own and sharing equality with man the responsibility for the development of society in all its aspects. This is the direction in which we shall have to move." The aim is providing educational and vocational training primarily to girls. Girls still face discrimination in getting an education in many parts of the world, even if there has been some limited progress in recent years, according to a UN report published, "Gender parity in education is a priority not only because inequality is a major infringement of fundamental human rights, but also because it represents an important obstacle to social and economic development."

Our Constitution provides for affirmative action by way of reservation so as to provide impetus to certain class of persons, who cannot reach the desired level of participation in public life and suffer from the handicap of social and educational backwardness. They require positive discrimination in their favour. Their population, social and educational standard and status have undergone a drastic change from a stated of bieng deprived of education civilised life backwardness, illiteracy and poverty. The best possible start in life for women is access to quality basic education, including free and compulsory primary education and ample opportunities for girl child and adolescents to develop their individual capacities. State governments should in implement programmes relating to all areas of girl child development. There is need for wider dissemination, and education can be used as the platform for human development and sharing of information on gender equality, campaigning against discrimination and advocating elimination of all sorts of discrimination.

Education and Tribal Economy

The problem of education among the tribals is related with their economic problems. Economic decisions are vital for any family. Some economic factors are responsible for lack of interest shown by the tribal people in getting education. Rural economy and family income very much depends upon the earning of each and every member of the family, so loss of each day earning affects the total income of the family. This also has an effect in attending the school and training programmes and official work, which hamper participation of elected members. A soon as the tribal attain the age of five or six, they become economic assets of the family and help in various economic activities of their parents. Varrier Elwin (1963) very appropriately sums up the situation in the following way, "For a tribal family, to send its grown-up girl or boy to school, is essentially a matter of economics; and entails dislocation in the traditional pattern of division of labour—may parents cannot just afford to send their children to school." The parents utilise their children's services for household needs. According to them, going to school means wasting time in unproductive pastimes. The tribal children substantially contribute to their family income through assisting their parents in the various economic activities like looking after the livestocks, house, children, and grown-up children look after the agricultural activities. Mere opening of more schools will not serve the desired purpose unless some economic incentive is provided to compensate for the loss, which these economically helpful hands render.

Since most of the tribal people are living in abject poverty under subsistence economy, it is not easy for most of them to send their children to schools, thus losing two healthy hands in their struggle for survival. It is clear that not much emphasis on education is given in rural areas. In fact, the tribals are economically dependent on the non-tribals and also educationally are weaker. The linkage between education and economy on the one hand and linkage between education and the social sector on the other hand are extremely important in understanding and shaping education. "Due to lack of value of education parents are not enthusiastic in sending their children to school. Most of the rural parents feel that when their grown-up children are in a position to add something to their family purse, there is no need to send them to school and incur double loss—losing the earning of the children on the one hand and spending the money for their education on the other hand.[20]

Concluding Observations

It is a proven fact that education plays a significant role in social development and this belief is not without any basis. Education ranks as an important impact of creating a social order founded on the values of freedom, social justice and equal opportunity. It is education that determines the level of prosperity, welfare and security of the people. Education may increase economic productivity and hence the earning power; it can improve the power of understanding, enabling a person to be better socialised and play his role in the society in a more satisfactory way, and it may in all probability enhance the cultural level of the people permitting them to enjoy the fruits of various arts. Most of the tribals believe that their children can progress only if they are educated and it will also be advantageous to their community. The goal and objectives of education at different stages and spheres are likely to be reoriented or structured. Programmes of educational reconstruction would constitute the major plank of educational policy. We need to modify our education system to promote lateral thinking and innovation. The spread of education should be taken as a social mission. There should be a an intensive effort towards exploring as to what will be the best possible way of doing it, which could also help in the mission of sharing of information on gender equality, campaigning against discrimination. It should be the destination for quality education in the entire country but just how effective it will be is a moot question.

References

1. Jagan Shankar (ed.), *Social Problem and Welfare in India,* Ashish Publishing House, New Delhi, p.263.
2. Indian Council of Social Science Statistical Organisation, *Social Information of India: Trends and Structure*, Hindustan Publishing Corporation, Delhi, 1983.
3. S.K. Saini, *Development of Education in India,* Cosmo Publications, New Delhi, 1980.
4. Parimal B. Kar, *Sociology the Discipline and its Dimensions*, New Central Book Agency, Calcutta, 1985, p. 282.
5. R.C. Mehrotra, *Education, Science and Human Values*, Wiley Eastern Limited, New Delhi, 1994, p.117.
6. Vimal P. Shah and Tara Patel, *Social Contexts of Tribal Education,* Concept Publishing Company, New Delhi, 1985, p.4.
7. I.L. Kandel, *Conflicting Theories of Education*, The Macmillan Company, New York, 1938, pp.78-79.
8. B. Kuppuswamy, *Social Change in India*, Vikas Publishing House, Ghaziabad (U.P.), 1984, p. 301.
9. Vimal P. Shah and Tara Patel, op. cit., p.159.
10. Nadeem Husain, *Tribal India*, Palka Prakashan, New Delhi, 1999.
11. Karen Birdsall, *Sociology*, Polity Press, U.K., 2000, p.523.
12. R.C. Mehrotra, *op.cit.,* p.119.
13. B. Kuppuswamy, op. cit., p.366.
14. Daniel Lerner, *The Passing of Traditional Society: Modernising the Middle East*, The Free Press, New York, 1968, p.55.
15. Ibid., p. 57.
16. Shuja Nawaz, *The Mass Media and Development in Pakistan*, Asian Survey, Vol. XXIII, No.8, Aug. 1983, p.936.
17. B. Kuppuswamy, op. cit., p.367.
18. Ibid., p. 368.
19. Indian Council of Social Science Research Central Statistical Organisation, Op.cit., 1983, p.119.
20. Jagan Shankar, op.cit.

6

Case Studies of some Elected Members

Case studies are good examples of getting knowledge about the action plans and programmes under way. Here are just a few illustrated.

1. Zila Pramukh (Sh. Chhagan Lal Jain)

Researcher interviewed Sh. Chhagan Lal Jain, Zila Pramukh, Udaipur, who is from a Jain family from Salumber. Interview was taken on the subject on his affiliation with political party, regarding rights of Zila Pramukh, reservation and other varied subjects.

He is a member of the Congress Party since 35 years. He was Municipal Counsellor in Nagpur (Maharashtra) in 1966. Afterward he shifted to his native place and became Sarpanch of Jaitana Panchayat, Pradhan of Salumber Panchayat Samiti, Member of Udaipur Zila Parishad and then became Upa-Pramukh of Udaipur Zila Parishad. Finally, at the time of interview he was holding the position of Pramukh of Zila Parishad.

Regarding views on rights of Zila Pramukh he was clear on the subject. He told the researcher that a Zila Pramukh has only supervision power whereas administrative powers should also be with Zila Pramukh. His anger was clearly on the government policies where he said that the central government and state Government only talk about Panchayati Raj but Zila Pramukh, member of Zila Parishad and Panchayat Samitis are only showpiece. These should be made powerful with more rights but state ministers and MLA's do not want to give powers and rights to all the above positions. According to protocol a Zila Pramukh holds a higher position than a District Collector and is Zila Pramukh asked to prepare the Credit Report of District Collectors. Presently the Collector is empowered for every work. This clearly indicates that the government has no will-power to empower the elected member of Panchayati Raj institutions.

Regarding reservation of SC's & ST's and women, his views were that reservation should be based on the size of the population. He quoted the example of Mavli, Vallabh Nagar, Udaipur, Salumber and Gingla Panchayats where the population of general people is about 99 per cent but the Sarpanch is a tribal which creates problems socially. He further quoted that he was working for the betterment of the tribals since 1975, but giving them political reservation was no solution to their backwardness. They should be provided educational facilities with more affected implementation. Regarding women's reservation he was clear that education is an essential prerequisite for empowering them because they do not have any knowledge about the PRI's.

2. Pradhan (Smt. Nirmala Choudhury)

Smt. Nirmala Choudhury, Pradhan of Girva Panchayat Samiti, is a member of Kalal Community which falls is OBC category. She is a young dynamic woman of 36 years of age. She lives with her husband and two children in a nuclear family. A graduate, she had taught in a school before entering into active politics.

She was encouraged to enter politics by her husband, was an elected member of Udaipur Municipal Committee and presently holds an important post in Block Congress Committee. She took active part in the development of the area and accompanied Dr. Girija Vyas and Sh. Khemraj Katara, in many areas.

Regarding general people taking part in politics, she was of the opinion that except for government employees, everyone should take part in politics, so he will conscious about his rights and duties. Her views about reservation of tribals were that they are being benefited and should be continued but it should not be increased. There should be no reservation for tribal income tax payers and gazetted officers. Reservation for women is very essentials for their active participation and empowerment.

Approach roads, drinking water and irrigation facilities, primary health facilities are not adequate for the area; transport facilities and open sale of liquor are other problems, which should be tackled. Regarding educational facility she said there are lady teachers who could not attend schools regularly due to lack of approach roads which was hampering education in remote areas. No new school should be opened and all the schools should be provided with more facilities, light food should be provided to students to attract them and male teacher to be appointed in the remote areas.

The researchers is of the opinion that her level of education and deep involvement in tribal affairs and local area development has helped her in knowing about these institutions and understanding rules, regulations, procedures and problems of local people. She is happy to have become a member of development authority (Pradhan) wherein she has got a chance to serve the people. She is encouraged and attributes her success to the people of her area and her husband's active support.

3. Pradhan (Sh. Roop Lal Parmar)

Sh. Roop Lal Parmar, Pradhan of Sagwara Panchayat Samiti, is an influential tribal leader of 47 years. He lives in a nuclear family with his four family members. He owns five bighas of agriculture land irrigated by self-owned well.

He is affiliated to the Bharatiya Janata Party since 20 years in the area which is traditionally a Congress stronghold. He was Sarpanch before he became Pradhan of Sagwara Panchayat Samiti. He is a popular leader reputed for his work related with problems of local people.

When he was asked about the problem of local people, he complained about the drinking water with high percentage of fluoride and for this he told the researcher that there should be filtration plants. He further told that in the area there were no avenues of permanent employment, so the people of this area migrate to Maharashtra and Gujarat for jobs and the family members have to face many hardships. He is of the opinion that government should work on this problem. His views regarding reservation were that there is no need to increase reservation of the tribals but the present facility should be implemented effectively. Reservation to tribal gazetted officers and income tax payers should be discontinued but reservation to other sections of society should be given. NGO's should work on individual development for overall development of the area.

4. Pradhan (Sh. Bhagwan Lal Gameti)

Sh. Bhagwan Lal Gameti, Pradhan of Badgama Panchayat Samiti, is a young dynamic tribal leader of 36 years of age. He is a graduate and lives in a nuclear family with his four children and wife. He works with Jyoti Jan Vikas, an NGO as secretary. He is a member of the Congress Party since seven years. He was Ward Panch in the last Panchayat election. Before entering politics he worked with Sewa Mandir, an NGO and formed his own NGO with like-minded people His concern is called Jyoti Jan Vikas funded by Oxford India Trust, a UK -based funding agency. Jyoti Jan Vikas worked on problems of mine labourers in Khamnore mining area in Rajsamand district, which proved to be the platform for his entering politics.

He works on the problems of local people and is very enthusiastic to solve them. When the researcher went to interview him at about 7.30 a.m., she saw about 10-15 with him discussing the problems of their area and he was listening to them very patiently.

Regarding relief work he was of the opinion that it should be done on the projects of permanent nature, such as plantation, building of small dams and school buildings which would help the localls in the long term. Relief work done of a temporary nature are of sheer wastage of funds and manual labour and is the manipulation of data to be presented to the public as an eyewash. He further told that a committee of local people should be formed to assess and evaluate the work done by the Panchayats and governmental agencies.

Funds should be allotted according to the need and geographical conditions of the area. Regarding NGO's he said that people are unaware of them. So there are many difficulties in implementing the programmes.

Regarding reservation he was of the opinion that tribal gazetted officers should not be given any further reservation. Reservation of women in P.R.I.'s should be raised to 50 per cent, which would prove to be ladder for them to have high positions in politics. Education is not a prerequisite of politics but experience teach politics and P.R.I.'s are the best school.

5. Pradhan (Smt. Hantok Charpota)

Smt. Hantok Charpota, Pradhan of Garhi Panchayat Samiti, is a 30-years-old tribal woman. She lives in a nuclear family with her husband and three children. She has no formal education but can only sign her name. Her father-in-law, Devi Lal Charpata, was former Pradhan and presently Sarpanch, and has encouraged her to contest the election.

She takes each and every advice for the decision from her father-in-law who is a politically active member of the Congress party. While interviewing her it was observed that she is working as proxy to her family and the Congress party and was unable to takes every decision without consulting her family. But she had clear opinion that reservation of tribals was essential for the upliftment of the community in every sphere, i.e., education, politics and economics but reservation for tribal gazetted officers and income tax payers should be discontinued.

6. Sarpanch (Sh. Laxmi Lal)

Sh. Laxmi Lal, son of Sh. Rajmal, is Sarpanch of Makda Dev Panchayat in Jhadol Panchayat Samiti. He lives in a nuclear family with his two wives and a child, and owns four bighas of land, which is irrigated by self-owned well. His brother was Panch in the last Panchayat election. His father was against his contesting and entering politics, but he with the help of friends and the support of the BJP of which he was a member for the last ten years won the election. He is president of Jhadol Tehsil's Jan Jati Morcha and actively works for the BJP and the tribals of the area.

He is worried about the plight of the tribals and informed the researcher that many tribal families are converting to Christianity due to poverty. He is well informed about the NGO's working in the area.

Again on reservation his opinion is that the reservation for all gazetted officers and income tax payers should be discontinued and there should not be more that 33 per cent for women in general. All parties should make up their mind to provide reservation to women through a legislature which his party, i.e., BJP wanted to pass in the LokSabha. Tribals should be given reservation in army and defence services which will help them in gaining confidence of defending the interests of their country.

Regarding problems of his area he was of the opinion that there should be a check on felling of trees in the forest and there should be intensive plantation on the barren hills. Construction of anicut was a problem because the irrigation department does not lend ears to voice of the tribals. Tribals lack in education, so more new schools should be opened and the existing schools be upgraded.

The Researcher is of the opinion that Sh. Laxmi Lal is a young dynamic leader and works on solving the problems of the local people.

7. Sarpanch (Sh. Amba Lal)

Sh. Amba Lal son of Kishna Ji, Sarpanch of Badrana Panchayat in Jhadol Panchayat Samiti, is 34 years old and has received education up to 9th standard. He is a member of the Congress since 13 years. He lives in a nuclear family with his four children and wife, and owns five bighas of agricultural land irrigated by self -owned well. His uncle was Ward Panch and he was Ward Panch in the last Panchayat election.

His knowledge about the welfare schemes is updated as he mentioned all monetary assistance, i.e., in IRDP cases, a maximum of Rs. 10,000 is provided to S.T. as subsidy, in Indira Awas Rs.18 thousand is provided and for Kelu houses Rs. 10,000 is provided as assistance. He has full knowledge about the NGO's working in the area, i.e., Lok Jumbish, Sewa Mandir working on med bandi and adult education, Magra Vikas sponsored by forest department whose chairperson is Sarpanch of the area.

Regarding women's reservation he is of the opinion that 33 per cent reservation is all right but in Panchayats illiterate women are elected, so the Sarpanchs can work as they wish. He is an alert person and is fully aware of the problems of the local people.

He told the researcher that there was conversion in the past and there were 18 Christian families; now they have been reconverted to Hindus.

The researcher is of the opinion that experience makes the person well informed about the problems of the local area irrespective of education. So is the case of Sh.Amba Lal who, despite being less educated, is working wholeheartedly for the people of his area.

7

Findings and Suggestions

Human needs keep changing. It is very difficult to predict what the future holds and what steps can be taken to see that these needs are satisfactorily met. Many problems of development in rural and urban areas are interdependent. The Panchayati Raj institutions are local governments at the district and block levels. This is how they are conceived and constituted. Their purpose is to bring the popular government closer to the people.

It appears that the local bodies are neither fulfilling their basic responsibilities nor paying adequate attention to issues linked with basic civic amenities. To improve the working of the local self-government department along with the local bodies for achieving the goal of providing better civic amenities to citizens. Authorities in the local self-government department have more or less abdicated their responsibility and allowed the chaos to continue. It is very necessary for the government agencies to integrate various interrelated data, including socio-economic, to arrive at optimum solutions and alternative strategies to meet the needs of the local people. People, local authorities and government should pursue the implementation of plans and programmes, so that there can be a sustainable and durable development, which can be monitored regularly for making the plan successful. Cooperation from local officials, PRIs and people is very necessary.

The fundamental attribute of democracy is good governance and it cannot be separated from human rights, which include human dignity, justice, equity and participation. A.D. Benoist says "The highest measure of democracy is neither the 'extent of freedom' nor the 'extent of equality', but rather the highest measure of participation." It is too often said that the local self-government institutions have failed because of public apathy, in other words, because of lack of people's participation. "When leaders are effective, they give something and get something in return. This social exchange or transactional approach to leadership involves a trading of benefit."[1]

People's participation is the felt need of the times and is very much essential in the process of good governance and also is an essential part of political process. It is an assumption that PRIs must equip themselves with the help of the common people's participation to improve their administrative, social and economic performance, and this assumption will be a reality when central and state governments and administration implement policies through PRIs wholeheartily. It also appears to be the sign of the effective role played by PRIs in growing awareness among common people for the decisive role played by them in development of societies, and of the determination of people to assume greater responsibility for their own future, with knowledge of what is at stake and what is good for their betterment and development. The objective of good governance and all-round governance can be better achieved if central and state governments with the help of government officials and machinery generate and inspire confidence among common, people especially rural tribal and women.

In this chapter an attempt is made to examine and evaluate the understanding of PR leaders about the concept of Panchayati Raj, its goal, and the points of its success and failure, and on their basis recommendations on ways and means for effective planning are made. Panchayati Raj was introduced with a view to involve peoples' participation through elected leaders in rural development. Men are judged as they are, and institutions will be judged by what men make of them. In addition to this, it entails to enquire from the leaders under study and analyse their priorities of development schemes, their ambition structure about rural development in their areas, their views about the impediments in the development work, the attempts they have made to remove the hindrances that come in the way of village development and their views about their participation in the planning rural development.

On her visit to these tribal areas and on interviewing a number of male and female members, on the basis of different scenarios and from analysis and interpretation of the data as well as from the result of various components the author drew the following conclusions. On the whole, the picture is uneven but it would be too pessimistic to draw a dismal picture all round because there are bright spots here and there and it would be unrealistic to deny them. We are now seeing tremendous growth to be a major source of new employment by creation of rural infrastructure like irrigation, water harvesting structures, roads, primary health centres and primary schools. Taking account of their cultural diversity, lifestyle, standard of living, income and communication facilities appear to be the key elements in a rural development strategy. The main focus of our research has been to study and examine the role of rural (tribal) members in the Panchayati Raj institutions. The tribals including women through reservation policy introduced by the Rajasthan government are given opportunity to enter the local political institutions, which is followed by the other states.

We see that tribals played a vital role in the Independence struggle but were not given their due regard and rights. After Independence political parties started to think about the welfare of tribals but it was more for their political gain and tribals were not benefited as shown in their manifestoes and the papers. This can be seen when we study the struggle of tribals for their entity, which has resulted in tribal states. The tribals of Rajasthan could not organise themselves and lagbehind in the development process.

On the basis of the results of the study some suggestions are made which may be helpful in women's participation and involvement in decentralized governance more effective and in strengthening Panchayati Raj system in the state.

Tribals were not allowed to participate in the political process of the country. With Independence and the equal rights granted by the Constitution it raised the tribals' status to some extent. Political empowerment, i.e., giving tribals the capacity to influence the decision-making process by integrating them into our political system was the main concern of the Panchayati Raj Act. The tribals and rural folk should not only become beneficiaries of development but also more importantly be contributors to the development process. The analysis of various aspects, based on data collected in regard to participation of tribals, was that their number has increased but they have not been able to affect decision making more due to lack of awareness. Awareness building among the people needs to be given top priority because the success of decentralised planning depends on the people's involvement in the planning process. It is our social responsibility to create awareness and responsibility in society.

Education and Training

Education plays a decisive role in one's attitude, which is the mirror to one's mind and reflects one's thinking. Attitude is an inherent part of one's personality and has an impact on the people, working environment and family life. Education changes the attitude to all about being proactive to the effect of bad incident because one cannot control what happens to one, but one can control one's attitude towards what happens to one. It is a catalyst in the positive thought process, which can be applied in day-to-day life. Illiteracy often comes in the way of ensuring human rights of all individuals, so we have to make efforts and a beginning in this desired direction. Every person would be able to get his piece of cake only through political awareness and an active participation in the public life, which is possible by education.

The government has shown all concern for the development of literacy in free India. Adult education is not only an action plan but is a multidisciplinary and cross-cultural approach to the study of social action.

In view of the poor standard of literacy and poor enlightenment in various matters, it is desirable that members should be instructed thoroughly about their duties and functions. The comprehensive training programmes can improve upon the competence and capacities of rural leaders. Although there are training centres for members, a few days, training is not sufficient for them. Sometimes a refresher course is also held but that is organised rarely since government is always running short of funds. Besides training, members may be served with written instructions clearly pointing out their duties and rights, powers and functions. It is further suggested that a people's committee should be set up in every Panchayat to conduct resource mapping under the auspices of the elected Panchayat committees. Volunteers should be selected and given training for them in survey research and preparation of sector-wise status report. This will help the Panchayats to identify and realise the real demands of the Panchayats and availability of resources.

In the field survey we found that 22 female respondents out of 28 are literate, which means they can spell their names but are unable to read. Our countriy's educational policy is aimed only to increase literacy rate, it may be through adult education. Merely by writing one's name on a paper will not improve the mental level of a person nor can it improve the capacity of understanding. Sound basic education is fundamental to the strengthening of higher level of education and capacity and thus to self-reliant development. Education must involve community development programmes, which will bring changes in one's attitudes relying on self-change. This can be understood a by remark made at the World Education Forum, held at Dakar in Senegal in April 2000, "Education for all has to be about quality, not just filling in the classrooms." Better educational facilities should be made available in tribal areas. Government has assumed a larger responsibility to look after the integrated character of education, to look after the international aspects of education, culture and human resource development; in general to promote excellence in the sectors of education throughout the country. All illiterate person would not be able to understand all the rules and regulations governing the institutions of Panchayati Raj. Good governance is not limited to regulation but to a larger effort to put in practice, a sharp correction any time which is expected to show good results. These functions have not been effectively discharged due to lack of training of Panchayat members. To make the system work effective the mass has to be conscientised. Training should be given to the elected members on their roles and responsibilities. Education levels among the leaders tend to be diluted by substantial percentage of the elected being illiterate or semi-literate, particularly women and the Scheduled Castes and Tribes. Education is important for the development of tribals. This should be promoted through their mother tongue.

The rural man needs to know a minimum of law, governing judicial and administrative process as well as the powers of various state organs. Further, in recent decades, various political parties have sprung up in the rural area. These parties struggle among themselves to win the support of the rural people with a view to gaining control over the state. It is, therefore, also necessary for the rural people to study the programmes and policies of these political parties. Both these reasons make it obligatory for them to have education. Education promotes knowledge, values, attitudes and skills conducive to respect for human rights and to an active commitment to the defence of such rights, and to the building of a culture of peace and democracy. Educational development is a participatory process and it will help them to understand the rules, regulations and fulfil the objectives of Panchayati Raj institutions. It help them in carrying out their day-to-day functions and will also help in the development of personality, social mobility and change in occupation. Every person has in him the potential to excel, and all they have to do is to create a favourable environment. There are no failures in life but there are only learning experiences, so it is suggested that training courses should be organised to improve their performance. Human rights and duties are now the central focus in all educational plans.

In the tribal areas, the tribal population is the most oppressed and backward among the whole population of the country. Education was incorporated in the list of facilitate evaluation of all Indian policies in the field of education. The tribal leadership can be more effective by educating the people. If the population and leaders are educated it will accelerate their awareness and involvement in dealing with government officials. Most of the tribal Panchayat members lack awareness about their powers and duties provided in the Panchayati Raj Act. The government should impart training regarding their powers and duties, which can be defined as functional literacy. Education changes the attitude towards life, our outlook on relations between people and also between government, society and people. In order to achieve these aims, the strategies and forms of action of educatioal systems will clearly need to be modified, as necessary, in respect both of teaching and of administration. Mass media can also play a vital role in this regard. The infrastructure created by Panchayat Raj institutions can be utilised in a better way by training and motivating the Panchayati Raj personnel working in the tribal areas.

In the case of Panchayati Raj leaders, it can be observed that the commitment, dedication and involvement of elected leaders can play a vital role in educating the rural mass because the majority of people was illiterate and ignorant about their welfare. "No socio-economic change is possible without a suitable political structure to mobilise the local people and involve them in participatory work especially in a country of magnitude and complexities."[2]

There is so much of paper work in PRI's that if one does not know to read and write, one (elected member) will feel isolated and will also lose confidence. It is also felt by the researcher that they will be guided by other persons as per their wish. So it is suggested that there should be minimum qualification for contesting elections. To take advantage of the various development schemes, a certain degree of education is necessary. For the elected members in present

Panchayats separate training should be given to educate them about all government policies, their duties, their rights, and all government welfare schemes should be explained and above all, the budget sanctioned.

Training programmes being organised by governmental and non-governmental agencies for empowering women will all direct mainly towards improving their symbolic presence in the Panchayati Raj institutions. It is suggested that vocational training should be provided to the inmates of every home. Our experience has shown that a multidimensional approach towards family and community betterment with emphasis on education, skill development, income generation and women's development works more effectively than laws. They should be given proper training that they may learn how to plan and thus they play an important role. The knowledge should be imparted through seminars and discussions.

Instead of engaging themselves with the urgent political and socio-economic realities, our politicians and leaders use the suffering of people to step into the seat of power and their mere aim is to retain power. We should look at various steps to check them and their subsequent consequences. It is believed that every bit of success has to be earned. This is the time to share the basic objectives and work in the same direction based on the objective because these days success depends on each other rather than solely on oneself. We must be prepared to change our behaviour till we get what we want. The success in the face of heavy odds will be an inspiration to all who dream of freedom and would have a positive impact on the rest of the country. It should leave no one in doubt that economic reforms have created more possibilities of upward mobility. There have been times when we were involved in situations out of which there seemed no way and this created a general tendency to think on the negatives. We get into these situations not because we do things that are wrong, but because we approach our activities with divided intentions. We have to stop this scepticism and what is important for us is to keep the improvement intact and focus on the positives. This will create more opportunities. Education will help us believe in ourselves and approach everything with a whole heart and will always pull us through difficulties.

Health

Most of the villages in the TSP area have little and poor quality access to health care. If they are provided good and free health care this will help the population to be educated in family planning and will ultimately reduce population growth. Hence it is suggested that PHCs and health centres must be set up in every village equipped with trained personnel. Their attendance must be assured by leaving the implementation to the Panchayats and should be devolved with power to disburse salaries on assessment of work and attendance.

It is suggested that Public Distribution System should be vitalised so that the rural population get access to this system, because the shopkeepers in rural are adulterate the eatables and play with the health of the people. Governments have made no concerned effort to regenerate the health department in the rural areas, resulting in collapse of health services and poor health of the people. To improve the health services in the rural areas, the village community (through Panchayati Raj institutions) need to be involved in the supervision and functioning of the whole system to make accountable to the people.

The health status or sickness of a community, especially within a modern nation state is required to be understood according to the social conditions. The social conditions include access to the basic needs and amenities like food, drinking water, housing, education, employment, transport, communication, etc.

Government providing medical facilities to the rural and tribal population gives more stress on family planning, ignoring the health sector of the population. So the population has to depend upon the private and expensive medical facilities, which is burden on the rural and tribal populations. Disease syndromes have pushed the families of tribals towards persistent poverty. The people are not only deprived of basic health services but also other basic needs like proper food, drinking water, etc.

Due to geographical conditions of the TSP area it is very difficult for the people to get medical facilities, due to lack of inadequate infrastructural facilities and it is also difficult for the medical staff to provide medical facilities. It is recommended that the geographical situation must be taken into account and special planning should be given due importance.

Unfavorable environment in the segments, namely, agriculture, infrastructure, housing and health care affected the performance of government agencies and local bodies in rural areas, mainly tribal. The health problems need special attention in the context of rural areas and particularly in the context of the tribals, so the author has in mind some steps, which can be helpful in providing improved facilities to rural folk regarding their health. The medical and health infrastructure includes hospitals, primary health centres, dispensaries, special nutrition programme centres, family planning units, mobile medical units, etc. The health policy must give priority to rural areas by making requisite investment. The post of doctors and medical staff should be created in terms of geographical and health conditions of the people of the area, and health institutions in rural areas should be made functional by posting adequate staff, ensuring their presence during the working hours, availability of essential medicines, beds and other infrastructural requirements. Emergency services in the rural health centres should be provided by putting doctors on rotational duties and also providing ambulance services and transport facilities to the medical staff. Above all, to work out these steps, the strong will of the government is a prerequisite. All the PRIs should be asked to promote awareness about the importance of nutrition and hygiene so that a healthy life could be promoted. The nutrition needs should be linked with some income-generating activities so that the nutritional needs could be properly implemented.

ROADS

The connected roads have definitely been an important catalyst in the development of the area. It would enable the administration to have a better control and supervision over all local institutions and developmental programmes. All manufactured goods and agricultural products need transportation, many by road. The citizen would be given ample opportunity to avail of adequate resources, which are available to provide the best civic amenities and essential services. Huge geographical areas and difficult topography of Rajasthan necessitate greater expenditure on the maintenance of law and order and prevention and investigation of crimes. The state plan should envisage expansion and strengthening of infrastructure and utilisation of information technology at all levels.

HOUSING

Tribal society is traditionally a nuclear family society, which can be observed in the research. It is due to that in every family when a boy is married he is given a house built for him and is separated from the day he is married. This plays a great role in the economic condition and development because land and other belongings are also divided among the family members.

Housing is one sector of tribal life which is not very gloomy as the land owned by the family is used as housing to some extent and land for agriculture becomes less. Particularly in the plains, some are landless and homeless and their plight is really miserable. So the researcher is of the opinion that they should be assured of better and cheaper housing facilities on a large scale sponsored and financed by the government on the land demarcated for the use of dwelling.

LAND HOLDING AND INCOME

The process of land alienation must stop and agriculture should be given a boost through improved inputs better techniques and developed machines and equipment. The true potential of Indian agriculture can be realised only when we can diversify our agricultural products, both geographically and over time. It is necessary to evolve a new approach to agricultural policy based on a careful assessment of current constraints and possibilities. A sober and careful assessment of our resources indicates that both land and water will be crucial constraints on our efforts to expand production in agriculture.

Modernising agriculture has meant an increase of technological inputs in the land and the tools of agriculture rather than investment in the people who own this agricultural land. We have to do many things to remove the apprehensions of the farmers; it includes modernisation of agriculture, repairs of roads, construction of checkdams, sinking of deep borewells, improvement of degraded forestland. It is recommended that at the time of district planning, geographical situation must be taken into account and special planning should be given due importance. In the absence of improvement in economic growth due to lower agricultural growth and growing inequalities in the distribution of income, in the face of reduced employment growth as well as deterioration in the quality of employment, a decisive expansionary policy is necessary. "In conclusion it may be said that educated unemployment becomes a source of social, economic and political discontent and turmoil in the country."[3]

Steps should be taken to increase the average income of tribal and for this, it is very necessary that appropriate measures for the development of agriculture should be taken. In the absence of improvement in economic due to lower agricultural there will be no growth in the income of tribal people through family and beneficiary oriented schemes of socio-economic development. The government should frame and implement policies and diversification programmes with view to generate more and more employment opportunities, these efforts should be taken with multiple objectives of improving the employment avenues and improving state and national economy.

Finance

"If the local bodies are to play any significant part in economic and social development they must clearly have access to the adequate finance."[4] "Finance has been accepted as a life-blood of Panchayati Raj institutions as they have to perform mainly the task of socio-economic development of the community."[5]

On the financial aspect the PRIs should be on a firm footing and for this these institutions should be encouraged and given power to generate their own resources. Inadequacy of financial powers has been hampering the process of democratic decentralisation. Members are not paid travelling allowance, or any honorarium. Although members may not be paid any salary due to various reasons of which paucity of fund is one, it is desirable that they should be paid some allowance at least. It is said that public service is a thankless job, and very few people would like to devote their time and energy for public cause. Besides, if members of parliament and legislative assemblies can be entitled to monthly pay and pension, why not the members of local bodies at the grass roots level?

Women

Women Panchayat members could not play their role due to various social, economic and psychological problems. The involvement of women representatives at the village level is negligible—in attending the meetings, expressing their views, interactions with officials and in decision-making process. They are merely dummy representatives and are not independent in taking any type of decisions—regarding their family, Panchayat and society. The vast majority of tribal women living in the far-flung pockets of the country are engaged in agriculture and forestry, agriculture including ancillary pursuits like animal husbandry, horticulture, etc,. In a way, even forestry is ancillary to agriculture. The Five-year Plans must also focus on increasing work opportunities and productivity of women farmers. Increasing women's access to productive land by regularising leasing and sharecropping of uncultivated agricultural land by women's groups, encouraging collective efforts in bringing wastelands under cultivation and providing policy incentives to women in low-input subsistence agriculture, will have immediate benefits in terms of household, food, security and women's empowerment.

In tribal societies, women play a bigger social and economic role than in the non-tribal societies. Women in the tribal areas generally enjoy greater freedom—in the choice of life-partners, in the dissolution of marriage, widow-remarriage, and even in attire and food habits. Women are barred from a number of ceremonial recreational activities. This is possible as there is no law for the protection of rights of the tribal women in any of the state.

Women have poor representation at the parliamentary and state legislative level. The 73rd and 74th Amendments of the Constitution mandated one-third reservation of seats for women in all local level elected bodies. As a result women in the rural areas participated in political matters in a big way and at the level of the Panchayati Raj institutions also the progress has been varying and fluctuating. This is mainly because of the uninterrupted and undisturbed dominance of the rural elite, i.e., the patriarch of the rural power structure. Rural people have long-ranging perception of the bases of leadership as is evident from their answers to the schedules. Hopefully, the Panchayats of the seventy-third constitutional amendment will place in their hands a direct institution, which they can use for devising their own plans and programmes as well as the tools for their implementation.

Women's participation in Panchayati Raj system was found to be quite low due to male dominance. There is a strong need for attitudinal change among the males as well as among the females of our society. As Mahatma Gandhi said, "Woman is not helpless, she must never regard herself as weaker than man. She should not, therefore, beg for any man's mercy, nor depend on him."[6]

It is evident that the women perform an important role in the economic life of the tribes. In tribal society, women shoulder heavy the responsibility of maintaining their respective families side by side with their male partners. Women's work is of much more importance as they participate in farming and animal husbandry work besides attending to household duties. Despite their important economic role they do not stand on par with men, because they feel they were not economically independent, for going to attend meetings and for going outside the village, they have to ask their husbands for money, even for the bus fare. As illiteracy was the main hurdle in women's participation in the Panchayati Raj, their educational standard should be enhanced for their better performance in the system. Despite the government's desire to provide adequate education facilities through reservation and other incentives for the educational development of the tribals, the result is not satisfactory and all have failed to attract, specially the girls.

Despite having a woman Prime Minister, India could not provide opportunities to women in the Lok Sabha. When we see the number of women in the parliament since 1952, in 1977 there were only 10 women members, this being the lowest and the 1984 election brought the highest number of women in the parliament which was 44 but when we see it percentage wise it was only 8 per cent of the total strength of parliament.

Women occupy an important place in contemporary India, marked by tradition and modernity. To be equal partners in the national development, the women of India should be provided with the facilities of education, employment and health. Looking at the employment patterns today, we see that women are concentrated in the limited range of jobs. Over half of the employed women in India are to be found in agriculture, which is less income generating. Women are poorly represented in areas such as science, engineering, Technology and management. The diversity and importance of the economic and social roles played by tribal women has been exhorting the scientists and specialists. The government of India has been giving much attention to science and technology programmes ever since its-independence. This can be achieved only by the strong will of the government to implement the various legislatures relating to these basics of the overall development. The problem of integrating tribal women in the development process is now engaging the attention of planners and policy makers all over the country. Our progress on social and economic fronts will not be achieved if we leave tribals, especially tribal women for from the main stream. Women should be considered as an equal partner in the implementation of the action programmes.

There is need for affirmative and real action in favour of women which will ensure for women the right to food, shelter, health, education and employment. Women should play a dominant role in shelter and sanitation programmes, as they are generally enthusiastic in such programmes. The present scenario is kindling hopes for the future. It must be realised that there is need for transfer of technology to women so as to improve production and efficiency and reduce drudgery in the occupation of farming. Despite the law, we are not able to give a square deal to our women, mainly the tribal women.

Political participation, whether by women or by men, is a function of numerous variables. There was actually no determined or organised effort on the part of the leaders of the movements to enrol women activists. It was quite natural in a male-dominated society. Though women have become members of political parties, their percentage is very low. When the question of closeness to a political party comes the picture is not too encouraging. It is usually found that in the case of a women candidate, the election campaign is conducted mainly by party workers among whom women usually form a small minority.

Reservation

The policy of reservation stands, at least in the short run, as an integral part of the process of socio-economic change and development in India. Reservation is an important tool for eradicating poverty but communities are also oppressed to educate themselves and finally compete on an equal basis with others.

Women represent half of the world's population and a majority of them are engaged in work that contributes to the life and economical status of their family. Women in India traditionally have faced, and continue to face, many forms of violence simply because they are women. They still face many obstacles in their fight for representation. They may be politically active, but once married, they disappear from the political scene.

Providing reservation for women has not effectively enabled women to participate in the decision-making process through Panchayats. To gain their rightful place in every field of activity there is a long struggle ahead of them.

About the reservation of women the author agreed with the view of Sh. Bhagwan Lal Gameti, Pradhan, Badgama that Panchayati Raj institutions are good training grounds for women to emerge as good and capable leaders who could bear the responsibilities that usually come along with higher political positions.

Accountability

The broad goals of tribal development should be well defined and their achievement should become timebound, coupled with the administrative responsibility and accountability. This is a vain hope because it presupposes that there would be a similar insistence on accountability and transparency in all walks of life, civilian as well as military. This unfortunately runs counter to what passes for Indian political culture. Accountability must be strengthened. The Gram Sabha is envisaged to play a significant role in providing for people's participation in the Gram Panchayat activities. It is also intended to ensure transparency in decisions and actions of the Panchayat, thereby strengthening its public accountability.

The functioning of institutions depends on the enforcement of the legislature. For enforcement of the legislature defaulters should be made accountable by law. Unless politicians, political parties and bureaucrats are made fully accountable for their misdoing and are booked for inefficiency in their respective areas of action there will be no possibility of improvement. Nobody, whosoever he may be, should be allowed to escape responsibility, and if politicians and bureaucrats with their political clout are allowed to get by with their misdeeds, the basic fabric of democracy will be jeopardised. The Gram Sabha should list out priorities and assist in the selection of beneficiaries for various programmes and schemes. In this way, the aspirations of the people would be articulated.

A mass awareness drive among the officials and common people should precede the implementation of law and policies formulated by the government. People can examine their own personal condition and human conditions generally with respect to the character of their liberties, and can recognise and evaluate the effects of the governmental policies and programmes. The people are the best judge of what concerns them.

The policies formed by the government for the welfare of the common people or for the some specified group or community should be considered as the fundamental rights of the person for whom the policy is being formed and could be challengable in the court of law. Governmental and its machinery should be liable for prosecution. Awareness building among the people needs to be given top priority because the success of elected members depends on the people's involvement in the planning process. It has been observed that very little had been achieved and much more remains to be done. The author is of the opinion that maximum well being in the population can be achieved if individuals are allowed to plan their own activities according to their needs.

References

1. Edwin P. Hollander, *Leadership Dynamics*, The Free Press, New York, 1978, p.7.
2. K. Shastri, *Political Linkage and Rural Development*, National Publishing House, New Delhi, 1976, p.8.
3. Lucy Mair, *An Introduction to Social Anthropology*, Oxford University Press, London, 1972, p.187.

4. U.K. Hicks, *Development from Below*, The Clarendon Press, Oxford, 1961, p.227.
5. Shamser Singh Malik, *The New Panchayati Raj*, Aalekh Publishers, Jaipur, 2002.
6. *The Times of India,* No.20, Vol. CLXII, January 23, 1999.

Annexure I

The Constitution (Seventy-Third Amendment) Act, 1992

[20th April. 1993.]

An Act further to amend the Constitution of India

BE It enacted by Parliament in the Forty-third Year of the 'Republic of India as follows:

1.1) This Act may be called the Constitution (Seventy-third Amendment) Act, 1992.

2) It shall come into force on such date as the Central Government may, by notification in the Official Gazette, appoint.

2. After Part VIII of the Constitution, the following Part shall be inserted, namely:

PART IX
THE PANCHAYATS

243. In this Part, unless the context otherwise requires,

a) "District" means a district in a State;

b) "Gram Sabha" means a body consisting of persons registered in the electoral rolls relating to a village comprised within the area of Panchayat at the village level;

c) "intermediate level" means a level between the village and district levels specified by the Governor of a State by public notification to be the intermediate level for the purposes of this Part;

d) "Panchayat" means an Institution (by whatever name called) of self-government constituted under article 243B, for the rural areas;

e) "Panchayat area" means the territorial area of a Panchayat;

f) "population" means the population as ascertained at the last preceding census of which the relevant figures have been published;

g) "village" means a village specified by the Governor by public notification to be a village for the purposes of this Part and includes a group of villages so specified.

243A. A Gram Sabha may exercise such powers and perform such functions at the village level as the Legislature of a State may, by law, provide.

243B.1) There shall be constituted in every State, Panchayats at the village, intermediate and district levels on accordance with the provisions of this Part.

2) Notwithstanding anything in clause (1), Panchayats at the intermediate level may not be constituted in a State having a population not exceeding twenty lakhs.

243C.1) Subject to the provisions of this Part, the Legislature of a State may, by law, make provisions with respect to the composition of Panchayats:

Provided that the ratio between the population of the territorial area of a Panchayat at any level and the number of seats in such Panchayat to be filled by election shall, so far as practicable, be the same throughout the State.

2) All the seats in a Panchayat shall be filled by persons chosen by direct election from territorial constituencies in the Panchayat area and; for this purpose, each Panchayat area shall be divided into territorial constituencies in such manner that the ratio between the population of each constituency and the number of seats allotted to it shall, so far as practicable, be the same throughout the Panchayat area.

3) The Legislature of a State may, by law, provide for the representation:

   a) of the Chairperson of the Panchayat at the village level, in the Panchayats at the intermediate level or, in the case of a State not having Panchayats at the intermediate level, in the Panchayats at the district level;

   b) of the Chairpersons of the Panchayats at the intermediate level, in the Panchayats at the district level;

   c) of the members of the House of the people and the members of the Legislative Assembly of the State representing constituencies which comprise wholly or partly a Panchayat area at a level other than the village level, in such Panchayat;

   d) of the members of the Council of State and the members of the Legislative Council of the State, where they are registered as electors within-

      i) a Panchayat area at the intermediate level, in Panchayat at the intermediate level;

      ii) Panchayat area at the district level, in Panchayat at the district level.

4) The Chairperson of a Panchayat and other members a Panchayat whether or not chosen by direct election from territorial constituencies in the Panchayat area shall have the right to vote in the meetings of a Panchayats.

5) The Chairperson of

a) a Panchayat at the village level shall be elected in such manner as the Legislature of a State may, by law, provide, and

b) a Panchayat at the intermediate level or district level shall be elected by, and from amongst, the elected members thereof.

243D.1) Seats shall be reserved for-

a) the Scheduled Castes; and

b) the Scheduled Tribes, in every Panchayat and the number of seats so reserved shall bear, as nearly as may be, the game proportion to the total number of seats to be filled by direct election in that Panchayat as the population of the Scheduled Castes in that Panchayat area or of the Scheduled Tribes in that Panchayat area bears to the total population of that area and such seats may be allotted by rotation to different constituencies in a Panchayat.

2) Not less than one-third of the total number of seats reserved under clause (1) shall be reserved for women belonging to the Scheduled Castes or, as the case may be, the Scheduled Tribes.

3) Not less than one-third (including the number of seats reserved for women belonging to the Scheduled Castes and the Scheduled Tribes) of the total number of seats to be filled by direct election in every Panchayat shall be reserved for women and such seats may be allotted by rotation to different constituencies in a Panchayat.

4) The offices of the Chairpersons in the Panchayats at the village or any other level shall be reserved for the Scheduled Castes, the Scheduled Tribes and women in such manner as the Legislature of a State may, by law, provide:

Provided that the number of offices of Chairpersons reserved for the Scheduled Castes and the Scheduled Tribes in the Panchayats at each level in any State shall bear, as nearly as may be, the same proportion to the total number of such offices in the Panchayats at each level as the population of the Scheduled Castes in the State or of the Scheduled Tribes in the State bears to the total population of the State:

Provided further that not less than one-third of the total number of offices of Chairpersons in the Panchayats at each level shall be reserved for women.

Provided also that the number of offices reserved under this clause shall be allotted by rotation to a different Panchayat at each level.

5) The reservation of seats under clauses (1) and (2) and the reservation of offices of Chairperson (other than the reservation for women) under clause (4) shall cease to have effect on the expiration of the period specified in article 334.

6) Nothing in this Part shall prevent the Legislature of a State from making any provision for reservation of seats in any Panchayat or offices of Chairpersons in the Panchayats at any level in favour of backward class of citizens.

243E. 1) Every Panchayat, unless sooner dissolved under any law for the time being in force, shall continue for five years from the date appointed for its first meeting and no longer.

2) No amendment of any law for the time being in force shall have the effect of causing dissolution of a Panchayat at any level, which is functioning immediately before such amendment, till the expiration of its duration specified in clause (1).

3) An election to constitute a Panchayat shall be completed—

a) before the expiry of its duration specified in clause (1);

b) before the expiration of a period of six months from the date of its dissolution:

Provided that where the remainder of the period for which the dissolved Panchayat would have continued is less than six months, it shall not be necessary to hold any election under this clause for constituting the Panchayat for such period.

4) A Panchayat constituted upon the dissolution of a Panchayat before the expiration of its duration shall continue only for the remainder of the period for which the dissolved Panchayat would have continued under clause (1) had it not been so dissolved.

243F. 1) A person shall be disqualified for being chosen as, and for being, a member of a Panchayat

a) if he is so disqualified by or under any a for the time being in force for the purposes of elections to Legislature of the State concerned:

Provided that no person shall be disqualified on the ground that he is less than twenty-five years of age, if he has attained the age of twenty-one year.

b) if he is so disqualified by or under any law made by the Legislature of the State.

2) If any question arises as to whether a member of a Panchayat has become subject to any of the disqualifications mentioned in clause (1), the question shall be referred for the decision of such authority and in such manner as the Legislature of a State may, by law, provided.

243G. Subject to the Provision of this Constitution, the Legislature of a State may, by law, endow the Panchayats with such powers and authority as may be necessary to enable them to function as institutions of self-government and such law may contain provisions for the devolution of powers and responsibilities upon Panchayats at the appropriate level, subject to such conditions as may be specified therein, with respect to—

a) the preparation of plans for economic development and social justice;

b) the implementation of schemes for economic development and social justice as may be entrusted to them including those in relation to the matters listed in the Eleventh Schedule.

243 H. The Legislature of a State may, by law—

a) authorise a Panchayat to levy, collect and appropriate such taxes, duties, tolls and fees in accordance with such procedure and subject to such limits.

b) assign to a Panchayat such taxes, duties, tolls and fees levied and collected by the State Government for such purpose and subject to such condition and limits;

c) provide for making such grants-in-aid to the Panchayats from the Consolidated Fund of the State; and

d) provide for constitution of such Funds for crediting all money received, respectively, by or on behalf of the Panchayats and also for the withdrawal of such moneys therefrom, as may be specified in the law.

243-1.1) The Governor of a State shall, as soon as may be within one year from the commencement of the Constitution (Seventy-third Amendment) Act, 1992, and thereafter at the expiration of every fifth year, constitute a Finance Commission to review the financial position of the Panchayats and to make recommendations to Governor as to—

a) the principles which should govern—

i) the distribution between the State and the Panchayats of the net proceeds of the taxes, duties, tolls and fees leviable by the State, which may be divided between them under this Part and the allocation between the Panchayats at all levels of their respective shares of such proceeds;

ii) the determination of the taxes, duties, tolls and fees which may be assigned to, or appropriated by, the Panchayats;

(iii) the grants-in-aid to the Panchayats from the Consolidated Fund of the State;

b) the measures needed to improve the financial position of the Panchayats;

c) any other matter referred to the Finance Commission by the Governor in the interests of sound finance of the Panchayats.

2) The Legislature of a State may, by law, provide for the composition of the Commission, the qualifications which shall be requisite for appointment as members thereof and the manner in which they shall be selected.

3) The Commission shall determine their procedure and shall have such powers in the performance of their functions as the Legislature of the State may, by law, confer on them.

4) The Governor shall cause every recommendation made by the Commission under this article together with an explanatory memorandum as to the action taken thereon to be laid before the Legislature of the State.

243 J. The Legislature of a State may, by law, make provisions with respect to the maintenance of accounts by the Panchayats and the auditing of such accounts.

243K.1) The superintendence, direction and control of the preparation of electoral rolls for, and the conduct of, all elections to the Panchayats shall be vested in a State Election Commission consisting of a State Election Commissioner to be appointed by the Governor.

2) Subject to the provisions of any law made by the Legislature of a State, the conditions of service and tenure of office of the State Election Commissioner shall be such as the Governor may by rule determine:

Provided that the State Election Commissioner shall not be removed from his office except in like manner and on the like grounds as a Judge of a High Court and the conditions of service of the State Election Commissioner shall not be varied to his disadvantage after his appointment.

3) The Governor of a State shall, when so requested by the State Election Commission, make available to the State Election Commission such staff as may be necessary for the discharge of functions conferred on the State Election Commission by clause (1).

4) Subject to the provisions of this Constitution, the Legislature of a State may, by Law, make provision with respect to all matters relating to, or in connection with, elections to the Panchayats.

243 L. The provisions of this Part shall apply to the Union territories and shall, in their application to a Union territory, have effect as if the references to the Governor of a State were references to the Administrator of the Union territory appointed under article 239 and references to the Legislature or the Legislative Assembly of a State were references, in relation to a Union territory having a Legislative Assembly, to that Legislative Assembly:

Provided that the President may, by public notification, direct that the provisions of the Part shall apply to any Union territory or part thereof subject to such exceptions and modifications as he may specify in the notification.

243M.1) Nothing in this Part shall apply to the Scheduled Area referred to in clause (1), and the tribal areas referred to in clause (2), of article 244.

2) Nothing in this Part shall apply to—

a) the States of Nagaland, Meghalaya and Mizoram;

b) the hill areas in the State of Manipur for which district Councils exist under any law for the time being in force.

3) Noting in this Part—

a) relating to Panchayats at the district level shall apply to the hill areas of the District of Darjeeling in the State of West Bengal for which

Darjeeling Gorkha Hill Council exists under any law for the time being in force;

b) shall be construed to affect the functions and powers of the Darjeeling Gorkha Hill Council constituted under such law.

4) Notwithstanding anything in this Constitution,—

a) the Legislature of a State referred to in sub-clause (a) of clause (2) may, by law, extend this Part to that State, except the areas, if any, referred to in clause (1), if the Legislative Assembly of that State passes a resolution to the effect by a majority of the total membership of that House and by a majority of not less than two-thirds of the members of that House present and voting;

b) Parliament may, be law, extend the provisions of this Part to the Scheduled Areas and the tribal areas referred to in clause (1) subject to such exceptions and modifications as may be specified in such law, and no such law shall be deemed to be an amendment of this Constitution for the purposes of article 368.

243N. Notwithstanding anything in this Part, any provision of any law relating to Panchayats in force in a State immediately before the commencement of the Constitution (Seventy-third Amendment) Act. 1992. which is inconsistent with the provisions of this Part, shall continue to be in force until amended or repealed by a competent Legislature or other competent authority of until the expiration of one year from such commencement, whichever is earlier;

Provided that all the Panchayats existing immediately before such commencement shall continue till the expiration of their duration, unless sooner dissolved by a resolution passed to that effect by the Legislative Assembly of that State or in the case of a State having a Legislative Council, by each House of the Legislature of the State.

243 O. Notwithstanding anything in this Constitution,

a) the validity of any law relating to the delimitation of constituencies or the allotment of seats to such constituencies made or purporting to be made under article 243K, shall not be called in question in any court;

b) no election to any Panchayat shall be called in question except by an election petition presented to such authority and in such manner as is provided for by or under any law made by the Legislature of a State;

3. In clause (3) of article 280 of the Constitution, after sub-clause (b), the following sub-clause shall be inserted, namely:—

"(bb) the measures needed to augment the Consolidated Fund of a State to supplement the resources of the Panchayats in the State on the basis of the recommendation made by the Finance Commission of the State;"

4. After the Tenth Schedule to the Constitution, the following Schedule shall be added, namely:

ELEVENTH SCHEDULE

(ARTICLE 243G)

1. Agriculture, including agricultural extension.
2. Land improvement, implementation of land reforms, land consolidation and soil conservation.
3. Minor irrigation, water management and watershed development.
4. 'Animal husbandry,' dairying and poultry.
5. Fisheries.
6. Social forestry and farm forestry.
7. Minor forest produce.
8. Small scale industries, including food processing industries.

9. Khadi, village and cottage industries.
10. Rural housing.
11. Drinking water.
12. Fuel and fodder.
13. Roads, culverts, bridges, ferries, waterways and other means of communication.
14. Rural electrification, including distribution of electricity.
15. Non-conventional energy sources.
16. Poverty alleviation programme.
17. Education, including primary and secondary school.
18. Technical training and vocational education.
19. Adult and non-formal education.
20. Libraries.
21. Cultural activities.
22. Market and fairs.
23. Health and sanitation, including hospitals, primary health centres and dispensaries.
24. Family welfare.
25. Women and child development.
26. Social welfare, including welfare of the handicapped and mentally retarded.
27. Welfare of the weaker sections, and in the particular, of the Scheduled Castes and the Scheduled Tribes.
28. Public distribution system.
29. Maintenance of community assets

Annexure II

The Gazette of India
Extraordinary

PART-II—SECTION 1

PUBLISHED BY AUTHORITY

No.70 New Delhi, Tuesday, December 24, 1996/Pausa 3, 1981

Separate paging is given to this Part In order that It may be filed as a separate compilation.

Ministry of Law and Justice

(Legislative Department)

New Delhi, the 24th December, 1996/Pausa 3, 1918(Saka)

The following Act of Parliament received the assent of the President on the 24th December, 1996 and hereby published for general information:—

The provisions of/the panchayats (extension to the scheduled areas) Act, 1996

No. 40 OF 1996

[24th, December, 1996]

An Act to provide for the extension of the previsions of Part IX of the Constitution relating to the Panchayats to the Scheduled Areas.

Be it enacted by Parliament in the forty-seventh Year of the Republic of India as, follows:

1. This Act may be called the Provisions of the Panchayats (Extension to the Scheduled Areas) Act (1996).
2. In this Act, unless the context otherwise requires, "Scheduled Areas" means, Definition, the Scheduled Areas as referred to in clause (1) of article 244 of the Constitution.
3. The provisions of Part IX of the Constitution relation to Panchayats are hereby extended to the Scheduled Areas subject to such exceptions and modifications as are provided in section 4.
4. Notwithstanding anything, contained under Part IX of the Constitution, the Legislature of a State shall not make any law under that Part which is inconsistent with any of the following features, namely:

a) a State legislation on the Panchayats that may be made shall be in consonance with the customary law, social and religious practices and traditional management practices of community resources;

b) a village shall ordinarily consists of a habitation or a group of habitations of a hamlet or a group of hamlets comprising a community and managing its affairs in accordance with traditions and customs;

c) every village shall have a Gram Sabha consisting of persons whose names are included in the electoral rolls for the Pachayat at the village level;

d) every Gram Sabha shall be competent to safeguard and preserve the traditions and customs of the people, their cultural identity, community resources and the customary mode of dispute resolution;

e) every Gram Sabha shall—

i) approve the plans; programmes and projects for

social and economic development before such plans, programmes and projects are taken up for implementation by the Panchayat at the village level;

ii) be responsible for the identification or selection of persons as beneficiaries under the poverty alleviation and other programmes.

f) every Panchayat at the village level shall be required to obtain from the Gram Sabha a certification of utilisation of funds by that Panchayat for the plans, programmes and projects referred to in clause (e);

g) the reservation of seats in the Scheduled Area at every Panchayat shall be in proportion to the population of the communities in that Panchayat for whom reservation is sought to be given under Part IX of the Constitution:,

h) the State Government may nominate persons belonging to such Scheduled Tribes as have no representation in the Panchayat at the intermediate level or the Panchayat at the district level:

Provided that such nomination shall not exceed one-tenth of the total members to be elected in that Panchayat;

i) the Gram Sabha or the Panchayat at the appropriate level shall be consulted before making the acquisition of land in the Scheduled Areas for development projects and before re-settling or rehabilitation person affected by such projects in the Scheduled Areas; the actual planning and implementation of the projects in the Scheduled Areas shall be coordinated at the State level;

j) planning and management of minor water bodies in the Scheduled Areas shall be entrusted to Panchayats at the appropriate level;

k) the recommendations of the Gram Sabha or the Panchayats at the appropriate level shall be made mandatory for grant of prospection license or mining lease for minor minerals in the Scheduled Areas;

l) the prior recommendation of the Gram Sabha or the Panchayats at the appropriate level shall be made mandatory for grant of concession for the exploitation of minor minerals by auction;

m) while endowing Panchayats in the Scheduled Area with such powers and authority as may be necessary to enable them to function as institutions of self-government, a State Legislature shall ensure that the Panchayats at the appropriate level and the Gram Sabha are endowed specifically with—

i) the power to enforce prohibition or to regulate or restrict the sale and consumption of any intoxicant;

ii) the ownership of minor forest produce;

iii) the power to prevent alienation of land in the Scheduled Area and to take appropriate action to restore any unlawfully alienated land of a Scheduled Tribe;

iv) the power to manage village markets by whatever name called;

v) the power to exercise control over money lending to the Scheduled Tribes;

vi) the power to exercise control over institutions and functionaries in all social sectors;

vii) the power to control over local plans and resources for such plans including tribal sub-plans;

n) the State Legislature that may endow Panchayats with powers and authority as may be necessary to enable them to function as institutions of self-government shall contain safeguards to ensure that Panchayats at the higher level do not assume the powers and authority of any Panchayat at the lower level or of the Gram Sabha;

o) the State Legislature shall endeavour to follow the pattern of the sixth Schedule to the Constitution while designing the administrative arrangements in the Panchayats at district levels in the Scheduled Areas.

5. Notwithstanding anything in Part IX of the Constitution with exceptions and modifications made by this Act, any provision of any law relation to Panchayats in force in the Scheduled Area immediately before the date on which this Act receives the assent of the President which is inconsistent with the provisions of Part IX with such excerptions and modifications shall continue to be in force until amended or repealed by a competent Legislature or other competent authority or until the expiration of one year from the date of which this Act receives the assent of the President:

Provided that all the Panchayats existing immediately before such date shall continue till the expiration of their duration unless sooner dissolved by a resolution passed to, that effect by the Legislative Assembly of that State or, in the case of a State having Legislative Council, by each House of the Legislature of the State.

K.L.MOHANPURIA

Secy. To the Govt. of India.

Annexure-III

Draft Declaration on the Rights of Indigenous People

The UN Working Group for Indigenous Population took up the task for drafting a universal Declaration of Indigenous People Rights in 1987. The process culminated in 1993, when a Draft Declaration of Indigenous People Rights was accepted by the Working Group. The draft was discussed at the Sub-Commission on the Prevention of Discrimination and Protection of Minorities in 1994and is presently before the commission on Human Rights.

According to observers, a Working Group of the Commission may be asked to examine the draft and recommended further action to the Commission and for approved to ECOSOC.

The text of the Draft Declaration that appears here is the final draft that was adopted at the 11th Session of the Working group in July, 1993.

Affirming that indigenous peoples are equal in dignity and rights to all other peoples, while recognising the right of all peoples to the different, and to be respected as such,

Affirming also that all peoples contribute to the diversity and richness of civilisation and cultures, which constitute the common heritage of humankind,

Affirming further that all doctrine, policies and practices based on or advocating superiority of peoples or individuals on the basis of national origin, racial, religious, ethnic or cultural differences are racist, scientifically false, legally invalid, morally condemnable and socially unjust,

Reaffirming also that indigenous peoples, in the exercise of their rights, should be free from discrimination of any kind,

Concerned that indigenous peoples have been deprived of their human rights and fundamental freedoms, resulting, *inter alia*, in their colonisation and dispossession of their lands, territories and resources, thus preventing them from exercising, in particular, their right to development in accordance with their own needs and interests.

Recognising the urgent need to respect and promote the inherent rights and characteristics of indigenous peoples, especially their rights to their lands, territories and resources, which derive from their political, economic and social structures and from their cultures, spiritual traditions, histories and philosophies,

Welcoming the fact that indigenous peoples are organising themselves for political, economic, social and cultural enhancement and in order to bring an end to all forms of discrimination and oppression wherever they occur,

Convinced that control by indigenous peoples over development affecting them and their lands, territories and resources will enable them to maintain and strengthen their institutions, cultures and traditions, and to promote their management in accordance with their aspirations and needs,

Recognising also that respect for indigenous knowledge, cultures and traditional practices contributes to sustainable and equitable development and proper management of the environment.

Emphasizing the need for demilitarisation of the lands and territories of indigenous peoples, which will contribute to peace, economic and social progress and development, understanding and friendly among nations and peoples of the world,

Recognising in particular the rights of indigenous families and communities to retain shared responsibility for the upbringing, training, education and well-being of their children,

Recognising also that indigenous peoples have the right freely to determine their relationships with States in a spirit of coexistence, mutual benefit and full respect,

Considering that treaties, agreements and other arrangements between States and indigenous peoples are properly matters of international concern and responsibility,

Acknowledging that the Charter of the United Nations, the International Covenant on Economic, Social and Cultural Rights and the International Covenant on Civil and Political Rights affirm the fundamental importance of the right of self-determination of all peoples, by virtue of which they freely determine their political status and freely pursue their economic, social and cultural development,

Bearing in mind that nothing in this Declaration may be used to deny any peoples their right of self-determination,

Encouraging States to comply with and effectively implement all international institutions, in particular those related to human rights, as they apply to indigenous peoples, in consultation and cooperation with the people concerned,

Emphasizing that the United Nations has an important and continuing role to play in promoting and protecting the rights of indigenous peoples,

Believing that the Declaration is a further important step forward for the recognition, promotion and protection of the rights and freedoms of indigenous peoples and in the development of relevant activities of the United nations system in this field,

Solemnly proclaims the following United Nations Declaration on the rights of indigenous peoples:

PART 1

Article 1

Indigenous peoples have the right to the full and effective enjoyment of all human rights and fundamental freedoms recognized in the Charter of United Nations, the Universal

Declaration to Human Rights and International Human Rights law.

Article 2

Indigenous individuals and peoples are free and equal to all other individuals and peoples in dignity and rights, and have the right to be free from any kind of adverse discrimination, in particular that based on their indigenous origin or identity.

Article 3

Indigenous people have the right of self-determination. By virtue of that right they freely determine their political status and freely pursue their economic, social and cultural development.

Article 4

Indigenous peoples have the right to maintain and strengthen their distinct political, economic, social and cultural characteristics, as well as their legal systems, while retaining their rights to participate fully, if they so choose, in the political, economic, social and cultural life of the State.

Article 5

Every indigenous individual has right to a nationality.

Part II

Article 6

Indigenous peoples have the collective right to live in freedom, peace and security as distinct peoples and to full guarantee against genocide or any other act of violence, including the removal of indigenous children from their families and communities under any pretext.

In addition, they have the individual right to life, physical and mental integrity, liberty and security of person.

Article 7

Indigenous peoples have the collective and individual right not to be subjected to ethnocide and cultural genocide, including prevention of and redress for:

a) Any action which has the aim or effect of depriving them of their integrity, liberty and security of person;

b) Any action which has the aim or effect of dispossessing them of their lands, territories or resources;

c) Any form of population transfer which has the aim or effect of violating or undermining any of their of their rights;

d) Any form of assimilation or integration by other cultures or ways of life imposed on them by legislative, administrative or other measures;

e) Any form of propaganda directed against them.

Article 8

Indigenous peoples have the collective and individual right to maintain and develop their distinct and characteristics, including the right to identify themselves as indigenous and to be recognised as such.

Article 9

Indigenous peoples and individuals have the right to belong to an indigenous community or nation, in accordance with the traditions and customs of the community or nation concerned. No disadvantage of any kind may arise from the exercise of such a right.

Article 10

Indigenous peoples shall not be forcibly removed from their lands or territories. No relocation shall take place without the free and informed consent of the indigenous peoples concerned and after agreement on just and fair compensation and, where possible, with the option of return.

Article 11

Indigenous peoples have the right to special protection and security in period of armed conflict.

States shall observe international standards, in particular the Fourth Geneva Convention of 1949, for the protection of civilian population in circumstances of emergency and armed conflict, and shall not:

a) Recruit indigenous individuals against their will into the armed forces and, particular, for use against other indigenous peoples;
b) Recruit indigenous children into the armed forces under any circumstances;
c) Force indigenous individuals to abandon their lands, territories or means of subsistence, or relocate them in special centres for military purposes.
d) Force indigenous individuals to work for military purposes under any discriminatory conditions.

Part III

Article 12

Indigenous peoples have the right to practise and revitalize their cultural traditions and customs. This includes the right to maintain, protect and develop the past, resent and future manifestations of their cultures, such as archaeological and historical sites, artifacts, designs, ceremonies, technologies and visual performing arts and literature, as well as the right to the restitution of cultural, intellectual, religious and spiritual property taken without their free and informed consent or in violation of their laws, traditions and customs.

Article 13

Indigenous peoples have the right to manifest, practise, develop and teach their spiritual and religious traditions, customs and ceremonies; the right to maintain, protect, and have access in privacy to their religious and cultural sites;

the right to the use and control of ceremonial objects; and the right to the repatriation of human remains.

States shall take effective measures, in conjunction with the indigenous peoples concerned, to ensure that indigenous sacred places, including burial sites, be preserved, respected and protected,

Article 14

Indigenous people have the right to revitalised, use, develop and transmit to future generations their histories, languages, oral traditions, philosophies, writing system and literatures, and to designate and retain their own names for communities, place and persons.

States shall take effective measures, whenever any right of indigenous peoples may be threatened, to ensure this is protected and also to ensure that they can understand and be understood in political, legal and administrative proceedings, where necessary through the provision of interpretation or by other appropriate means.

PART IV

Article 15

Indigenous children have the right to all levels and forms of education of the state. All indigenous peoples also have this right and the right to establish and control their educational systems and institutions providing education in their own languages, in a manner appropriate to their cultural methods of teaching and learning.

Indigenous children living outside their communities have the right to be provided access to education in their own culture and language.

States shall take effective measures to provide appropriate resources for these purposes.

Article 16

Indigenous peoples have the right to have the dignity and

diversity of their cultures, traditions, histories and aspirations appropriately reflected in all forms education and public information.

States shall take effective measures, in consultation with the indigenous peoples concerned, to *eliminate* prejudice and discrimination and to promote tolerance, understanding and good relations among indigenous peoples and all segments of society.

Article 17

Indigenous peoples have the right to establish their own media in their own languages. They also have the right to equal access to all forms of non-indigenous media.

States shall take effective measures to ensure that State-owned media duly reflect indigenous cultural diversity.

Article 18

Indigenous peoples have the right to enjoy fully all rights established under international labour law/national labour legislation.

Indigenous individuals have the right not to be subjected to any discriminatory conditions of labour, employment or salary.

PART V

Article 19

Indigenous peoples have the right to participate fully, if they so choose, at all levels of decision making in matters which may affect their rights, lives and destinies through representatives chosen by themselves in accordance with their own procedures, as well as to maintain and develop their own indigenous decision-making institutions.

Article 20

Indigenous peoples have the right to participate fully, if they so choose, through procedures determined by them, in devising legislative or administrative measures that it may affect them.

States shall obtain the free and informed consent of the peoples concerned adopting and implementing such measures.

Article 21

Indigenous people have the right to maintain and develop their political, economic and social systems, to be secure in the enjoyment of their own means of subsistence and development, and to engage freely in all their traditional and other economic activities. Indigenous peoples who have been deprived of their means of subsistence and development are entitled to just and fair compensation.

Article 22

Indigenous peoples have the right to special measures for the immediate, effective and continuing improvement of their economic and social conditions, including in the areas of employment, vocational training and retraining, housing sanitation, health and social security.

Particularly attention shall be paid to the rights and special needs of indigenous elders, women, youth, children and disabled persons.

Article 23

Indigenous peoples have the right to determine and develop priorities and strategies for exercising their right to development. In particular, indigenous peoples have the right to determine and develop all health, housing and other economic and social programmes affecting them and, as well as possible, to administer such programmes through their own institutions.

Article 24

Indigenous peoples have the right to their traditional medicines and health practices, including the right to the protection of vital medicinal plants, animals and minerals.

PART VI

Article 25

Indigenous peoples have the right to maintain and strengthen their distinctive spiritual and material relationship with the land, territories, waters and coastal seas and other resources which they have traditionally owned and otherwise occupied or used, and to uphold their responsibilities to future generation in this regard.

Article 26

Indigenous peoples have the right to own, develop, control and use the lands and territories, including the total environment of the lands, air, waters, coastal seas, sea-ice, flora and fauna and other resources which they have traditionally owned and otherwise occupied or used. This includes the right to the full recognition of their laws, traditions and costums, land tenure systems and institutions for the development and management of resources, and the right to effective measures by States to prevent any interference with, alienation of or encroachment upon these rights.

Article 27

Indigenous peoples have the right to the restitution of the lands, territories and resources which they have traditionally owned or otherwise occupied or used, and which have been confiscated, occupied, used or damaged without their free and informed consent. Where this is not possible, they have the right to just and fair compensation. Unless otherwise freely agreed upon by the peoples concerned, compensation shall take the form of lands, territories and resources equal in equality, size and legal status.

Article 28

Indigenous peoples have the right to the conservation, restoration and protection of the total environment and the productive capacity of their lands, territories and resources, as well as to assistance for the purpose from States and through international cooperation. Military activities shall not take place in the lands and territories of indigenous peoples, unless otherwise freely agreed upon by the peoples concerned.

States shall take effective measures to ensure that no storage or disposal of hazardous materials shall take place in the lands and territories of indigenous peoples.

States shall also effective measures to ensure, as needed, that programmes for monitoring and restoring the health of indigenous peoples, as developed and implemented by the peoples affected by such materials, are duly implemented.

Article 29

Indigenous peoples are entitled to the recognition of the full ownership, control and protection of their cultural and intellectual property.

They have the right to special measures to control, develop and protect their, sciences, technologies and cultural manifestations, including human and other genetic resources, seeds, medicines, knowledge of the properties of fauna and flora, oral traditions, literatures, designs and visual and performing arts.

Article 30

Indigenous peoples have the right to determine and develop priorities and strategies for the development or use of their lands, territories and other resources, including the right to require their States obtain their free and informed consent prior to the approval of any project effecting their lands, territories and other resources, particularly in connection with the development, utilisation or exploitation of mineral, water or other resources. Pursuant to agreement with the indigenous peoples concerned, just and fair compensation shall be provided for any such activities and measures taken to mitigate adverse environmental, economic, social, cultural or spiritual impact.

Article 36

Indigenous peoples have the right to the recognition, observation and enforcement of treaties, agreements and other constructive arrangements concluded with States or their successors, according to their original spirit and intent, and to have States honour and respect such treaties, agreements and other constructive arrangements. Conflicts and disputes which cannot otherwise be settled should be submitted to competent international bodies agreed to by all parties concerned.

PART VIII

Article 37

States shall take effective and appropriate measures, in consultation with the indigenous peoples concerned, to give full effect to the provisions of the Declaration. The rights recognised herein shall be adopted and included in national legislation in such a manner that indigenous peoples can avail themselves of such rights in practice.

Article 38

Indigenous peoples have the right to have access to adequate financial and technical assistance, from States and through international cooperation, to peruse freely their political, economic, social, cultural and spiritual development and for the enjoyment of the rights and freedoms recognised in this Declaration.

Article 39

Indigenous peoples have the right to have access to and decision through mutually acceptable and fair procedures for the resolution of conflicts and disputes with States, as well as to effective remedies for all infringements of their individual and collective rights. Such a decision shall take into consideration the customs, traditions, rules and legal systems of the indigenous peoples concerned.

Article 40

The organs and specialised agencies of the United Nations system and other intergovernmental organisations shall contribute to the full realisation of the provisions of this Declaration through the mobilisation, *inter alia*, of financial cooperation and technical assistance. Ways and means of ensuring participation of indigenous peoples on issues affecting them shall be established.

Article 41

The United Nations shall take the necessary steps to ensure the implementation of this Declaration including the creation of a body at the highest level with special competence in this field and with the direct participation of indigenous peoples. All United Nations bodies shall promote respect for and full application of the provisions of the Declaration.

Part IX

Article 42

The rights recognized herein constitute the minimum standard for the survival, dignity and well-being of the indigenous peoples of world.

Article 43

All the rights and freedoms recognized herein are equally guaranteed to male and female indigenous individuals.

Article 44

Nothing in this Declaration may be construed as diminishing or extinguishing existing or future rights indigenous peoples may have or acquire.

Article 45

Nothing in this Declaration may be interpreted as implying for any State, group or person any right to engage in any activity or to perform any act contrary to the Charter of the United Nations.

(Source: INDIGENOUS AND TRIBAL SOLIDARITY, Indian Confederation of Indigenous and Tribal Peoples (I C I T P), 3rd General Assembly Meeting, 1997, New Delhi, pp. 239-246.)

Bibliography

Abraham, Francis, Dynamics of Rural Leadership in Village India, Indian International, Allahabad, 1974.

Adams, James F., *Human Behaviour in Changing Society*, Holbrook Press, Inc, Boston, United States of America, 1973.

Adhikari, Sudeepta, *Political Geography,* Rawat Publications, Jaipur, 1997.

Anderson, C.A., Skeptical Note on the Relations of Vertical Mobility to Education, *American Journal of Sociology*, Vol. LXVI, No. 5, March, 1961.

Arora, Ramesh K., *Administration Change In India,* Alekh Publishers, Jaipur.

Bailey, Joe, *Indians and Intervention: Social Theory for Practice*, Routledge and Kegan Paul, London, 1980.

Baral, J.K., *Gender Politics*, Discovery Publishing House, New Delhi, 1990

Bardhan, A.B., *The Tribal Problem in India,* Communist Party of India Publications, New Delhi, 1973.

Basu Ashok Ranjan & Satish Nijhawan, *Tribal Development Administration In India*, Mital Publications, New Delhi, 1994.

____________ (ed.), *Tribal Development Administration in India,* Mital Publications, New Delhi, 1994.

Beer, Samuel H., *Modern Political Development*, Government Random House, New York, 1974.

Beteille, Andre, *Caste, Class and Power,* University of California Press Ltd., London, 1965.

Bhargava, B.S., *Grass Roots Leadership: A Study of Leadership in PRIs,* Ashish Publishing House, New Delhi, 1979.

Bhatt, G.D., *Emerging Leadership Pattern in Rural India-An Empirical Study,* M. D. Publication Pvt. Ltd., New Delhi, 1994.

Bhattacharjee, A.R., *Panchayati Raj and Block Area Development,* Printwell, Jaipur, 1993.

Birdsall, Karen, *Sociology,* Polity Press, U.K., 2000.

Bottomore, T.B., *Sociology a Guide to Problems and Literature,* Blackie and Son Ltd., Bombay, 1975.

Burman, B.K. Roy, *Indigenous And Tribal People*, Mital Publications, New Delhi, 1994.

Celine Rani, A., *Emerging Pattern of Rural Women Leadership in India,* Kalpaz Publications, New Delhi, 2002.

Census of India, 2001, Series-9, Rural-Urban Distribution of Population, *Rajasthan Provisional Population Totals,* Paper-2 of 2001.

Chaudhary, Budhadeb, Tribal Transformation in India, *Ethnopolitics and Identity Crisis,* Volume III, Inter India Publications, New Delhi, 1992.

Chaudhary, S. S., *Electricity and Tribal Economy,* Shiv Publishers Distributors, Udaipur, 1995.

Chaudhry, D.S., *Emerging Rural Leadership in an Indian State,* Manthan, Rohtak, 1981.

Coleman, James William Donald R. Cressey, *Social Problems*, Harper & Row Publications, New York, 1980.

Dalton, George, *Economic Development and Social Change*, Basic Book Inc. Publishers, New York.

Davis, Kinsley, *Human Society*, Surjeet Publications, New Delhi, 1981.

de Grazia, Alfred, *Political Behaviour,* The Free Press, New York Collier Macmilon Limited Londan, 1962.

Desai, A.R., *Rural Sociology in India,* Popular Prakashan Private Limited, Bombay, 1969.

Dharam Vir, *Tribal Women, Changing Spectrum in India,* Classical Publishing Company, New Delhi, 1990.

Dube Leela, *Studies on Leadership Village India, Emerging Pattern of Rural Leadership in South Asia,* Hydrabad National Institute of Community Development, 1965.

Dubey, Ashilesh, *Commercialisation of Education in India: Policy, Law and Justice,* A. P. H. Publishing Corporation, New Delhi, 1997.

Dubin, Robert, *Human Relations in Administration,* 3rd Edition, Prentice-Hall of India, Private Limited, New Delhi, 1970.

Dumont, Louis, *Homo Hierarchicus,* Vikas Publication, Bangalore, 1966.

Franco Fernando & Edward Mathias, Financing Panchayati Raj Institutions: The Lack of Political Will, *Social Action,* Vol.51, No.3, July-September, 2001.

Friedlander, Walter A., Robert Z. Apte, *Introduction to Social Welfare,* Prentice Hall, Inc., U.S.A., 1982.

Ghildial, Avneet Kumar, *Political Development in Ghildial,* Classical Publishing Company, New Delhi, 1994

Ghosh Ratna and George Kurian, Some Ambiguities in the Concept of Development, *The Indian Journal of Political Science,* Vol.40, No.2, June, 1979.

Giddens, Anthony, *Sociology, Polity Press*, Cambridge, U.K., 2002.

Gill, Rajesh, *Social Change in Urban Periphery,* Allied Publishers Limited, New Delhi, 1991.

Gopalan, C., Bani Tamber Aeri, Strategies to Combat Under Nutrition, *Economic And Political Weekly,* Vol.XXXIV, No.33, August 18-24, 2001.

Gosh, Bishwanath, The Manace of Educated Unemployment in Search of a Strategy, *Industrial Time,* January 12, 1973.

Goyal, S.K., The study of schedule caste students of collage eastern UP, Research Project sponsored by *Indian Council of Social Science Research*, New Delhi, 1973.

Gupta Dipankar (Ed), *Social Stratification*, Oxford University Press, New Delhi, 1991.

Gupta K.R. (Ed.), *Rural Development in India,* Atlantic Publishers and Distributors, New Delhi, 2003.

Gupta, G.P., *Administrative and Developmental Perspective in Tribal Landscapes,* Arihant Publishers, Jaipur, 1992.

Gupta, Mukta, *Women and Educational Development,* Sarup & Sons, New Delhi, 2000.

Hicks, U.K., *Development from Below,* The Clareandon Press, Oxford, 1961.

Hollander, Edwin P., *Leadership Dynamics,* The Free Press, New York, 1978.

Horton, Paul B. Gerald R. Leslie, *The Sociology of Social Problems,* Printice-Hall, Inc., United States of America, 1978.

Husain, Nadeem, *Tribal India,* Palka Prakashan, New Delhi, 1999.

Hymen, Herbert H., *Political Socialisation,* Amerind Publishing Co. Pvt. Ltd., New Delhi, 1959.

Indian Council of Social Science Statistical Organisation, *Social Information of India: Trends and Structure,* Hindustan Publishing Corporation, Delhi, 1983.

Intodia, S.L., *Transformation of Tribals in Rajasthan Through I.R.D.P.* (A Case Study), Mahaveer Printing Press, Udaipur, 1988.

Jaguaribe, Helio, *Political Development : A General Theory And Latin America—A Case Study*, Harper and Row Publishers, New York, 1973.

Jha Uma Shankar (Eds.), *Status of Indian Women Crisis and Conflict in Gender Issues,* Kanishka Publishers, Distributors, New Delhi, 1998.

Joseph, Sarah, Democratic Good Governance: New Agenda for Change, *Economic and Political Weakly,* Vol. XXXV, No-12, March 24-30, 2001.

Joshi, Y.G., *Development in Over Exploited Tribal Region,* Inter India Publications, New Delhi, 1990.

Kall, Rekha, Accessing Primary Education: Going Beyond the Classroom, *Economic and Political Weekly,* Vol. XXXVI, No. 2, January 13-19, 2001.

Kandel, I.L., *Conflicting Theories of Education,* The Macmillan Company, New York, 1938, pp. 78-79.

Kar, Parimal B., *Sociology the Discipline and its Dimensions,* New Central Book Agency, Calcutta, 1985.

Karmakar, Sumati, *The Better Half Mother, Sister*, Wives and Homemakers, Dominant Publishers and Distributors, New Delhi, 2001.

Kenneth George Ritzer C.W. Kammeyer Norman, R. Yetman, *Sociology: Experiencing A Changing Society,* Allyn and Bacon, Inc., United States of America, 1979.

Key V. O., Jr., *Public Opinion and American Democracy,* Knoph, New York, 1961.

Khanna, B.S., *Rural Local Government in India and Asia,* Deep and Deep Publications Pvt. Ltd., New Delhi, 1999.

Kothari, C.R., *Research Methodology, Methods and Techniques,* Wiley Eastern Ltd., New Delhi, 1986.

Kuhn, Berthold, *Participatory Development In Rural India,* Radiant Publishers, New Delhi, 1998.

Learner David, *The Passing of Traditional Society, Modernising the Middle East*, The Free Press, New York, 1968.

Lesly, Philops, *Handbook of Public Relations and Communications,* Jaico Publishing House, Mumbai, 2002.

M. N. Sriniwas, *Religion and Society among Coorgs of South Indian*, Ch. 5.

Mair, Lucy, *An Introduction to Social Anthropology,* Oxford University Press, London, 1972.

Majumdar, D.N., *Race and Culture of India,* Asia Publishing House. Bombay, 1961.

Malik, Shamser Singh, *The New Panchayati Raj,* Aalekh Publishers, Jaipur, 2002.

Marvick, Dwaine, *Political Decision Makers,* The Free Press a corporation Printed in the United States of America, 1961.

_____________ Political Decision Makers, The Free Press of Glencoe, U.S.A., 1961.

Mann, R.S., *Tribal of India ongoing Challenges,* M D Publications, New Delhi, 1996.

Maroo, Rushikesh, *Empirical Modes of Political Development: A Critique, The Indian Journal of Political Science,* Vol. XXXVII, No.1, January-March, 1976.

Mathur, N.N.G., *Problems of Tribal Education,* Shiv Publishers Distributors, Udaipur, 1994.

Mathur, P. C. (ed.), *Social and Economic Dynamics of Rajasthan Politics*, Aalekh Publishers, Jaipur, 1996.

Mehrotra, R.C., *Education, science and human values*, Wiley Eastern Limited, New Delhi, 1994.

Mehta Basant and Kiran Kothari, *Human Resource Development,* Discovery Publishing House, New Delhi, 1999.

______________Role of Banks in Women Development, Discovery Publishing House, New Delhi, 2003.

Mehta, P.C., *Tribal Rights,* Shiv Publications Distributors, Udaipur, 1996.

Mehta, S. R., *Emerging Pattern of Rural Leadership*, Wiley Eastern, New Delhi, 1972.

Menaria, Rajendra, *Leadership in Tribal Area and Development,* Illustrated Book Publishers, Jaipur, 1992.

Merton Robert K. and Robert Nisbet, *Contemporary Social Problems,* Harcourt Brace Jovanovich, Inc., New York, 1971.

Miglani, D.C., *Politics and Rural Power Structure,* Deep and Deep Publication, New Delhi 1993.

Mishra, Arti, *Women in Slums: Impact of Environmental Pollution,* Classing Publishing Company, New Delhi, 2004.

Mishra, Sweta, *Changing Pattern of District Administration*, Mital Publications, New Delhi, 1996.

Mital, M.C., *Tribal transformation in India,* Volume II, Inter-India Publications, New Delhi, 1992.

Mohanty, B. B., Land Distribution among Scheduled Castes and Tribes, *Economic And Political Weekly*, Vol. XXXVI, No.40, October 6-12, 2001.

Muhammad, Shan, *Education and Politics,* A.P.H. Publishing Corporation, New Delhi, 2002.

Narain Iqbal and P. C. Mathur, Political Development A Theoretical Construct Without Research Applications, *The Indian Journal of Political Science,* Vol. XLIII, No.2, April-June, 1982.

Naval, T. R., *Legally Combating Atrocities on Scheduled Castes and Scheduled Tribes,* Concept Publishing Company, New Delhi, 2004.

Nawaz, Shuja, The Mass Media and Development in Pakistan, *Asian Survey,* Vol. XXIII, No.8, Aug. 1983.

Noronha, Frederic, 'Who's Afraid of Radio in India?', *Economic And Political Weekly,* Vol. XXXV, No.38, September 16-22, 2000.

Pachauri, S K., *Dynamics of Rural Development in Tribal Areas,* Concept Publishing Company, New Delhi, 1993.

Panigrahi, P.K., *Political Elite In Tribal Society,* Commonwealth Publishers, New Delhi, 1998.

Pant, Niranjan, *The Politics of Panchayati Raj Administration,* Concept Publishing Company, Delhi, 1979.

Pareek Udai and S. K. Reddy, *Studies in Indian Rural Leadership—A Review,* Udai Pareek (Ed.), *Studies on Rural Leadership,* Behavioural Science Centre, Delhi, 1966.

Pareek, Vijadra Kumar, *Adult Education,* Himanshu Publications, New Delhi, 1992.

Parsons, Talcott, *Politics and Social Structure,* The Free Press, New York, 1969.

Pati R.N. & J. Dash, *Tribal And Indigenous People Of India: Problems And Prospects,* A P H Publishing Corporation, New Delhi, 2002.

Perumal, C.A., Regionalism And Political Development, *The Indian Journal of Political Science,* Vol. XLVIII, No.1, Jan-March 1987.

Pfeffer George & Deepak Kumar Behera, *Contemporary Society: Tribal Studies,* Concept Publishing Company, New Delhi, 1997.

Prabhakar, Vani, *Third World Sociology*, Dominant Publishers and Distributors, New Delhi, 1999.

Rai Haridwar and S.P. Singh, Panchayati Raj And The Citizen: The Myth of Participatory Democracy, *The Indian Journal of Public Administration*, Vol. XXI, No.3, July-September, 1975.

Raj Kumar (Ed.), *Women And Education*, Anmol Publications Pvt. Ltd., New Delhi, 2000.

Raj Singh, *Panchayati Raj Manual*, Anmol Publications Pvt. Ltd., New Delhi, 1996.

Rao, Digumarti Bhaskara, *Education For All Achieving the Goal*, APH Publishing Corporation, New Delhi, 2000.

Rao, G. Lokeshmana, *Internal Migration and Political Change in India*, National Publishing House, New Delhi, 1977.

Rayappa P. Hanumantha, R. Mutharayappa, *Backward and Welfare of Scheduled Caste and Scheduled Tribes in India*, Ashish Publishing House, New Delhi, 1986.

Reddy G. Sreenivasa & P. Shyamsunder Reddy, *Political Participation of Scheduled Tribe- case of Political Inequality*, Ashok Printers, Warangal, 1985.

Reddy, M. M. Krishna, *Marriage Population and Society*, Kanishka Publishers, New Delhi, 1998.

Report Of The Working Group For Empowering The Scheduled Tribes During The Tenth Five Year Plan (2002-2007), Government Of India, Ministry Of Tribal Affairs, New Delhi, July, 2001.

Riggs, F.W., *Bureaucracy and Political Development*, Princeton N. J. Princeton Univ. Press, 1963

Roat, Harish Chandra, *Tribal Settlement System and Development Strategy*, Himanshu Publications, Udaipur, 1987.

Roy, Ashine, *Human Rights of Women*, Rajat Publications, New Delhi, 2003.

Roy, Kalpna, *Women in Indian Politics*, Rajat Publications, Delhi, 1999.

Roy, P.K., *Problem of Unemployment*, Capital Publishing House, Delhi, 1983.

Sahay, K.K., *Dynamics and Dimensions of Tribal Societies: Regional and Indian Perspective,* Commonwealth Publishers, New Delhi, 1998.

Saini, S.K., *Development of Education in India,* Cosmo Publications, New Delhi, 1980.

Saurath, Vivek, *Dynamic of Rural Development,* Dominant Publishers and Distributors, New Delhi, 1999.

Saxena, D.R., *Tribal And the Law,* Deep and Deep Publication, New Delhi, 1997.

Schaefer, Richard T., *Sociology International Edition,* Mc Grow-Hill, Inc., New York, 1989.

Selitz Clair, et al, *Research Methods in Social Science,* Holt Rinehart and Winston Inc., New York, 1962.

Shah Vimal P. and Tara Patel, *Social Contexts of Tribal Education,* Concept Publishing House, New Delhi, 1984.

Shankar Jagan, (ed.) *Social Problem and Welfare in India,* Ashish Publishing House, New Delhi.

Sharma S. P. and A. C. Mital, *The Tribal Women in India,* Radha Publication, New Delhi, 1998.

Sharma S. Ram (Ed.), *Women And Education,* Discovery Publishing House, New Delhi, 1995.

Sharma, K.L., *Rural Society in India,* Rawat Publications, Jaipur, 1997.

Sharma, Renu, *Political Change And Status of Women,* University Book House Pvt. Ltd., Jaipur. 2000.

Sharma, S. R., *Rural Elite in India,* Sterling, New Delhi, 1979.

Sharma, Yogendra K., *History and Problems of Education,* Kanishka Publishers, Distributors, New Delhi, 2001.

Shastri, K., *Political Linkage and Rural Development,* National Publishing House, New Delhi, 1976.

Singh J.P., (Eds.), *Tribal Women And Development,* Rawat Publication, Jaipur, 1985.

______________ N. N. Vyas, Tribal Development: Past efforts and New Challenges, Himanshu Publications, Udaipur, 1989.

Singh, Anil Kumar, *Approach to Tribal Development,* Sarup & Sons, New Delhi, 1994.

Singh, K.P., *Tribal Development in India,* Upper Publishing House, New Delhi, 1988.

Singh, Kedar, *Rural Democratization*, Virmal, Ghaziabad, 1974.

Singh, Vijadra, *Panchayati Raj and Village Development,* Sarup and Sons, New Delhi, 2003. Volume-1, 2,3.

Social Action, *A quarterly review of Social Trends,* October-December, Vol. 51, No.4, 2001.

Soni, Jasprit Kaur, *Introspection of Tribal Development,* Sonali Publications, New Delhi, 2004.

____________, Tribal Women: Emerging New Elite, Tribe, Vol.31, No.3-4, 1999.

Sriniwas, M.N., *Social Change in Modern India,* Berkeley University of California Press, 1966.

____________, & Premlata Pujari, Indian Women Today Tradition, Modernity And Challenge, Kanishka Publishers, Distributors, New Delhi, 1996

Srivastav, H.C., *Dysfunctional Para-Politics and Elite Action in India,* Bhartiya Vidya Prakashan, Varanasi, 1967.

Sudhakar, V., *New Panchayati Raj System,* Mangal Deep Publication, Jaipur, 2002.

Sundram, K.V., *Urban and Regional Planning in India,* Vikas Publishing House Pvt. Ltd., New Delhi, 1977.

Swamy, Erragattu M., *Rural Poverty and Agricultural Labour,* Printwell, Jaipur, 1996.

Thakur, D.N., *Tribal Women,* Deep and Deep Publication, New Delhi, 1996.

Thakur, Devendra, *Rural Development and Political Leadership in India,* Deep and Deep Publications, New Delhi, 1986.

Townsend Lucy Forsyth (Ed.), *Women: A Global Perspective,* Anu Books, Meerut, 2001.

Tribal Women in India, Indian Anthropological Society, Calcutta, 1978.